reading
for survival
in today's
society

reading for survival in today's society

VOLUME ONE
MODULES 1-18

ANNE H. ADAMS
Professor of Education and Director, Duke University Reading Center

ANNE FLOWERS
Professor of Education and Chairman, Duke University Department of Education

ELSA E. WOODS
Reading Coordinator, Durham, North Carolina, Public Schools

Goodyear Publishing Company, Inc.
Santa Monica, California

Library of Congress Cataloging in Publication Data
Main entry under title:
Reading for survival in today's society.
    1. Reading—Addresses, essays, lectures.
I. Adams, Anne H.   II. Flowers, Anne.   III. Woods, Elsa E.
LB1050.R4116   428.4   77-24017
ISBN 0-87620-769-7 (v.1)
ISBN 0-87620-767-0 pbk.

Library of Congress Catalog Card Number: 77-24017
ISBN: 0-87620-767-0 (paper)   ISBN: 0-87620-769-7 (case)
Y-7670-6 (paper)   Y-7697-9 (case)
Current Printing (last number)
10 9 8 7 6 5 4 3 2 1

SHERRI BUTTERFIELD, *project editor*
KITTY ANDERSON, *designer and art director*
JOYCE KITCHELL, *cover illustrator*
A., B. J., AND D. L. HOOPES, *production artists*
SHIRLEY COLEMAN, *typesetter*

Printed in the United States of America

to Sharman for saying just the right things
and
to Hank for being so patient

acknowledgments

For assistance in writing this book, the authors are most grateful to the many **teachers** and **students** who encouraged us in developing the functional materials theory to improve reading; to **Sharman Hall** for her diligence as a research assistant; to **Jackie Ward**, who typed the final manuscript; and to **Bob Wilson**, who offered suggestions for material.

For permission to use material in this book, grateful acknowledgment is made to the following publishers, companies, and groups:

RJR Foods, Inc. For Hawaiian Punch Drink Mix, Chun King, My*T*Fine Instant Pudding, and Hawaiian Punch Fruit Punch labels. Courtesy of RJR Foods, Inc.

Warner-Chilcott Laboratories, division of **Warner-Lambert Company**. For Brondecon label.

The Clorox Company. For Clorox Bleach label, 1976.

Allstate Life Insurance Company. For Life Insurance Application form.

United States Government, Department of the Treasury, Internal Revenue Service. For U.S. Individual Income Tax Return, Short Form 1040A.

United Airlines. For excerpts from *United Airlines, Our Friendly Times, 50th Anniversary*, copyright © 1976.

A. H. Belo Corporation. For television schedule from *Dallas Morning News*, May 26, 1976.

Time-Life Books. For *Foliage Houseplants* order card.

Borden Chemical, division of **Borden, Inc.** For "Love, Elmer's" advertisement.

Charlotte Observer. For "Sunny" and "It'll Be a Mite Cooler" weather reports, April 9, 1976.

Los Angeles Times. For excerpts from weather reports of April 8-9, 1976. Information contained in the reports was provided by the National Weather Service and reprinted by permission of the *Los Angeles Times*, copyright © 1976.

State of North Carolina, Department of Motor Vehicles. For excerpts from *North Carolina Driver's Refresher Handbook of Traffic Laws and Highway Safety*, 1973.

University Publishing Service, division of **Marketing Corporation of America**. For Duke University campus map and map of main routes to Duke University campus.

City of Durham, North Carolina, Chamber of Commerce. For excerpts from *Self-Guide Tour and Accommodations Directory*, revised September 1975; "Information List—Accommodations Through Churches"; and map and index of shopping centers, September 17, 1974.

Eastern Air Lines Incorporated. For excerpts from "Leave It All Behind for a Weekend" brochure, produced in August 1975 for use until December 15, 1975.

Lion Country Safari. For "The Village" and "The Preserve" excepts from Lion Country Safari brochure.

Random House, Inc. For excerpts from pronunciation key and page 106 of the *Random House College Dictionary*, revised edition, copyright © 1975 by Random House, Inc.

General Telephone Company of the Southeast. For excerpt from the 1976 telephone directory, Durham, North Carolina.

Kerr Drugs. For Application for Employment form.

Wachovia Bank & Trust Company, N.A. For excerpts from *Wachovia Practice Check Book*, revised 1973, and *Wachovia Checking Account* 3462, revised 1974.

Denver Chamber of Commerce. For excerpt from "Denver Business," 1975, page 3.

State of North Carolina, Department of Revenue. For excerpts from North Carolina Individual Income Tax Return, Form D-400, and "Instructions for Filing North Carolina Individual Income Tax Return, Form D-400," revised July 1, 1975.

State of Oregon. For diagram of "Steps in Enacting a House Bill in the Oregon Legislative Assembly" from *Oregon's Legislature and Legislative Process 1975-76*, pages 18-19.

State of Idaho, Department of Law Enforcement. For excerpts concerning motorcycle safety standards and requirements.

United States Department of Agriculture, Food and Nutrition Service. For list of publications, 1976.

Social Security Administration. For application for Social Security Card, Form SS5, September 1975.

contents

introduction

about survival reading

A growing national concern is being expressed for students who cannot read and write well enough to complete the most basic forms; and all educators, regardless of their disciplines, are feeling some of the increased pressure exerted on schools to graduate literate citizens. A recent newspaper article described the difficulties one person had paying his electric bill. In desperation the utility company finally wrote a letter admonishing him to pay the *amount*, not the *date*.

This incident, though humorous, illustrates the seriousness of the problem we face. The person unable to read his electric bill is representative of many persons in our society who are functionally illiterate. To meet their urgent needs, we must direct our attention to those areas of reading that are basic to everyday living and necessary for survival in today's society.

Theory

Survival or functional reading is essential reading, practical reading, the kind of reading a person must do daily to acquire the information needed to make life's decisions and meet society's demands. Traditionally, this kind of reading has not been a recognized part of school curricula although millions of persons cannot read accurately and respond successfully to printed material.

Survival reading realistically faces the fact that some types of reading, such as that done to understand and pay an electric bill, are not recreational or fun but are essential for effective communication and effective living. In survival reading instruction, the emphasis is on widening students' exposure to ideas in print and familiarizing them with the different styles and formats in which printed ideas appear. There is no controlled vocabulary. Students are encouraged to tackle unusual or difficult words, such as *condiment* and *intestate*, as they encounter them in survival reading contexts. Survival reading lessons make practical reading—the type of reading that directly affects our health and determines our future—seem as important as it is.

Instruction in survival reading can be started in the first grade with simple materials, such as one- and two-word direction and identification signs (WALK–WAIT or DON'T WALK, IN–OUT, ENTRANCE–EXIT, STOP–GO, GIRLS–BOYS). It should be started no later than the fifth grade and continued as needed throughout a student's elementary and secondary education. It can be invaluable to adults for whom English is a second language.

Materials

Survival reading materials come in all sizes, shapes, and colors. They are the stuff of daily communication. They range in content from coupons to contracts and in complexity from on/off indicators to step-by-step directions. They include maps and manuals, signs and schedules. Because their vocabulary has not been preselected, students find them challenging. They are as readily available as newspapers, magazines, and telephone directories. Their value lies in their interest-stimulating variety and their direct applicability.

There are no prescribed academic boundaries on the teaching of survival reading: it can be taught as a separate course or in conjunction with other content areas. Teachers who modernize, as well as individualize, basic instruction will find that survival reading materials become an essential part of their lesson plans and an enriching ingredient in reading programs and in English, mathematics, science, and social studies classes. Such materials bridge the gap between theory and practice and help students realize the relevancy and applicability of their education.

About This Book

Format

Reading for Survival in Today's Society was originally written as a single 36-module volume intended to be a resource book for teachers and a text for students for a 36-week course in functional reading. Because of its bulk, it has been divided into two smaller volumes of 18 modules each.

When the book was divided, the existing manuscript was not simply split in half. Instead, much thought was given to selecting the subject matter for each volume. Although the 36 modules were written to be used together, we sought to divide them so that teachers wishing to purchase only one volume could find one precisely suited to their needs. In selecting modules for Volume One, we considered what survival reading subjects and materials might naturally complement and supplement school curricula. Among the modules in this volume are ones dealing with current events, weather reports, dictionary skills, and city, state, and national government information. The modules in Volume Two are based on materials with which adults must cope: consumer information, apartment leases, ads for home furnishings, automobile purchase contracts, bills, credit cards, postal service forms, and food purchase and preparation information.

While individual students may find some modules more challenging than others, they were neither written nor arranged to form a necessary progression and may be used in any order—or out of order.

Purposes

The three major purposes of this book and its companion volume are:
- To provide students with an opportunity to develop and refine the skills necessary to read and interpret the printed matter they encounter in everyday living.
- To provide teachers with a sampling of the different kinds of printed materials basic to reading in today's society.
- To develop through comparison of past and present the idea that daily reading requirements are constantly changing.

In essence, the books are intended to help teachers decrease the number of students who cannot cope effectively with the print in their lives. Together, these books confront students with more than 120 different examples of the kinds of print they are likely to come across and be crossed up by, such as labels, leases, directions, schedules, tax forms, and bills. And they serve as a resource center for teachers, who rarely have enough time to put together so extensive and varied a collection of printed materials.

These books are *not* intended to teach students how to read a specific label or schedule, advertisement or application form. Rather, representative examples of such materials are used to help students develop the specific survival reading skills they will need to interpret print in any form and format.

Content

Each self-contained survival reading module is about ten pages long and includes:

- introductory text;
- a Survival Reading Skills section of questions based on printed material and selected to help students develop five specified skills;
- a list of Other Ideas for activities;
- a list of twenty Key Words and Phrases;
- a Self-Evaluation checklist.

INTRODUCTORY TEXT. The introductory text is on a page by itself, the first page of each module, and is intended primarily for teachers. In it we use sometimes startling statistics to underscore the importance of developing the reading skills demanded by the module's subject matter, list the specific survival reading skills the module is designed to develop, and suggest easy-to-obtain materials that might be collected, written for, or brought from home to supplement those in the module itself.

SURVIVAL READING SKILLS. The Survival Reading Skills section within each module consists of questions and reproductions of actual printed matter. With few exceptions, the questions relate to the reading material reproduced within the module. Because reading involves both comprehending and evaluating printed matter, these questions are of two types: (1) *basic factual questions*, for which the student must locate and fill in specific information, for example, the name of the state in which a product is made; and (2) *interpretive questions*, requiring him to apply this information or to express an opinion based on his background knowledge. Allow time for students to discuss their answers to the interpretive questions, either as a class or in small groups. Point out the wide range of possible answers and some of the reasons answers may vary. An Answer Key appears at the back of the book.

OTHER IDEAS. Each module includes a list of five to ten Other Ideas for activities to supplement the basic reading lessons. Designed to spark student creativity, these activities can best be done with a partner or in a small group. While some explanation may be needed to get students going, they should be encouraged to complete the activities chosen or assigned on their own.

KEY WORDS AND PHRASES. Also included in each module is a list of twenty Key Words and Phrases related to the module topic and found frequently in functional reading contexts. These words may be used as a pretest to assess the survival reading vocabulary of individual students or of the class as a whole. Where appropriate, they should be incorporated in classroom conversations and discussions and might be used:

- for spelling lessons
- to discuss multiple definitions
- to practice alphabetizing
- to practice dictionary skills
- in syllabication lessons
- in prefix and suffix lessons
- in antonym and synonym lessons

SELF-EVALUATION. A Self-Evaluation checklist appears on the last page of each module. For each skill activity in a module, the student should:
- record the date the activity was completed;
- record his or her score, that is, the number of correct answers;
- compare this score with the possible score;
- use this comparison to rate himself expert, average, fair, or in need of help.

For each module completed, the student should:
- record the date the module was completed;
- total the number of correct responses for all five skill activities;
- compare this score to the possible score for the entire module;
- use this comparison to rate himself or herself expert, average, fair, or in need of help;
- circle the letters of the Other Ideas completed.

ANSWER KEY. Answers for all basic factual questions are listed in the Answer Key. Because responses to interpretive questions will differ, the words "Answers will vary" appear in the key for these questions. Where appropriate, sample responses are provided for those questions for which a number of answers might be correct. We decided to put the Answer Key for each module at the back of the book, rather than within the module itself, so that teachers can control access to the key and can decide which answers should be checked first by students, and which ones should be checked first by the teacher.

No apology is offered for the topics in this book. Although we are committed to encouraging students to read stories, novels, and textbooks, we are very much aware that another kind of reading experience must be emphasized also if the number of functionally illiterate adults is to decrease. Interestingly, the functionally illiterate reader, in many instances, is not a remedial reader in other reading situations. Extremely bright people have difficulty comprehending information on internal revenue tax forms, home and automobile purchase contracts, and insurance policies.

This book serves as an introduction to contemporary functional reading. The information in it directly or indirectly affects us all. We have written it because we believe the greatest single gift a teacher can give a student is the ability to cope with the print he or she will encounter during a lifetime.

Anne H. Adams
Anne Flowers
Elsa E. Woods

reading for survival in today's society

labels

1

1

LABELS

Each year millions of labels are printed, placed on items, and displayed for people to read. They come in various sizes and shapes and carry an amazing assortment of information. At one time the information on labels could be highly distorted and make unsubstantiated claims for the product. Now regulations are fairly strict, and the label should accurately represent the product's ingredients and its intended use or purpose. Where the product may be toxic, the label should so state and describe the antidote, if any.

Students should learn to locate pertinent information on labels and to utilize this information in making purchases wisely and using products safely.

Specific reading lessons emphasized in this module are: (1) noting essential information on medicine labels; (2) identifying different kinds of information on a label; (3) finding warnings/cautions on labels; (4) reading basic information on labels; and (5) comparing information on different labels.

materials

In addition to this module's collection of labels, students should bring to class cans, jars, boxes, and other containers that have labels.

survival reading skills

1. NOTING ESSENTIAL INFORMATION ON MEDICINE LABELS
Read the **Brondecon** label and answer the following:

a. After what date should this medicine *not* be taken? _____

b. How many tablets should a person over 12 years of age take a day?

_____

c. If you become ill after taking this medicine and think it may be because of the medicine (adverse reaction), where do you look for information that tells you what to do?

_____

_____

d. Do you have to have a physician's prescription to take this medicine?

_____ Why? _____

_____

2. IDENTIFYING DIFFERENT KINDS OF INFORMATION ON A LABEL
Read the **Clorox** label and answer the following questions:

a. Which two rooms in the house might be cleaned with Clorox?

(1) _____

(2) _____

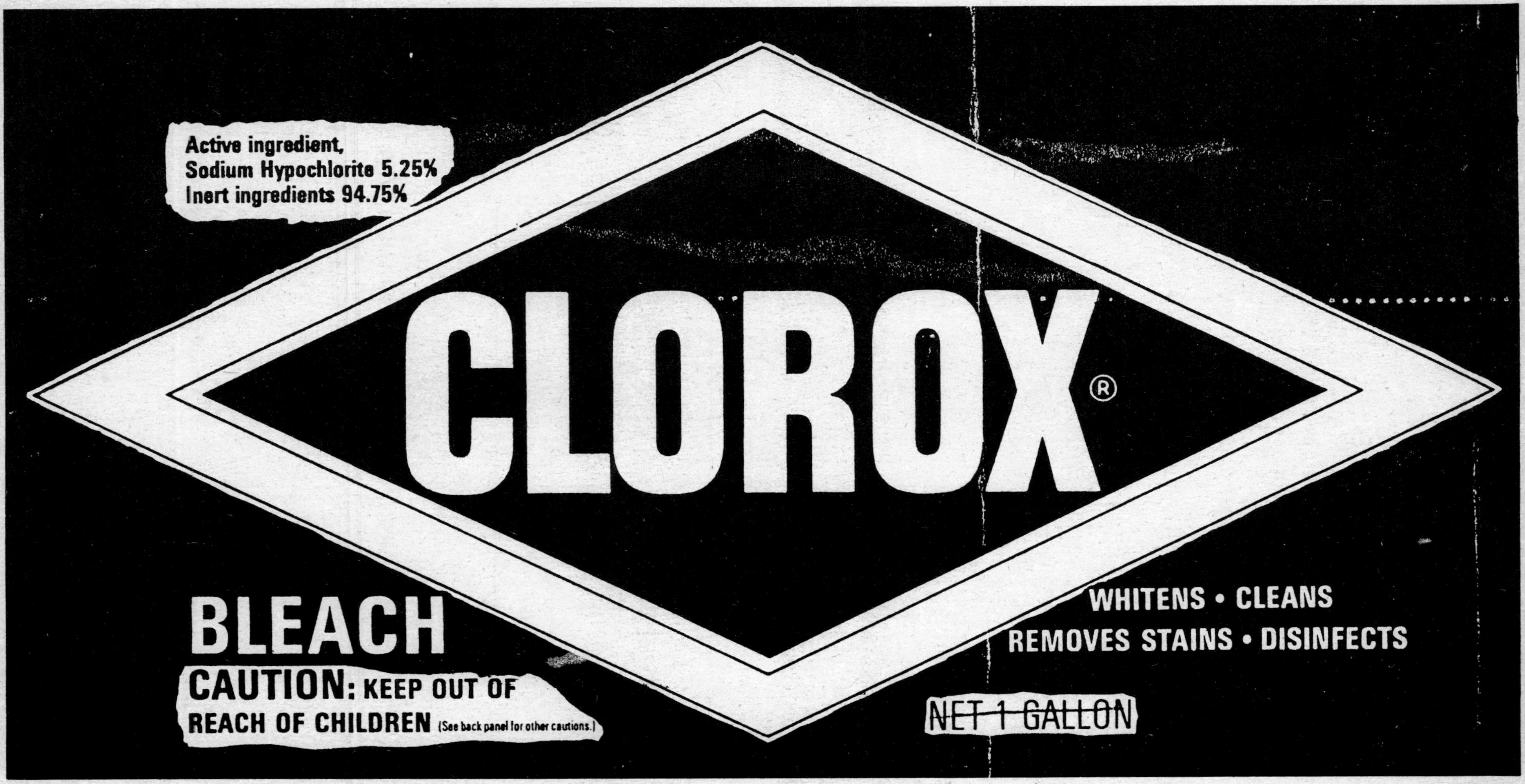
Active ingredient,
Sodium Hypochlorite 5.25%
Inert ingredients 94.75%
CLOROX®
BLEACH
CAUTION: KEEP OUT OF REACH OF CHILDREN (See back panel for other cautions.)
WHITENS • CLEANS
REMOVES STAINS • DISINFECTS
~~NET 1 GALLON~~

WHAT HOUSEHOLD CLEANING JOBS CAN CLOROX DO?

Use Clorox to clean your bathroom and kitchen. Clorox is economical, yet unsurpassed for disinfecting and deodorizing. Clorox cleans by removing stubborn stains and eliminating germ-caused odors from surfaces all around the house.

Toilet bowls—Pour in 1/2 cup of Clorox. Brush entire bowl. Let stand 10 minutes; flush. Do not use Clorox with toilet bowl cleaners. See caution statement.

Kitchen sinks—Cover stains with water. Pour 1/2 cup of Clorox directly into standing water. (Clorox will not remove rust or pot marks.)

Floors, vinyl or ceramic tile, woodwork, and kitchen appliances—Clean with a solution of 3/4 cup Clorox per gallon of sudsy water. (Do not use on cork.)

Bathtubs and showers—Clean with a solution of 3/4 cup Clorox per gallon of warm water.

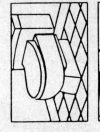

0   4 4600 00104

EVERY DETERGENT NEEDS CLOROX.®

For the broad range of laundry problems you encounter, no other type of additive used with your detergent can give a cleaner, brighter wash while disinfecting too.

DIRECTIONS FOR USE

HOW MUCH CLOROX SHOULD YOU USE?
To get the best cleaning results, you should use the proper amount of Clorox in the wash water. If too little is used, stubborn dirt and stains that detergent alone cannot remove may be left in and whites and colored fabrics may not stay as white and bright as possible.

The guidelines below should provide excellent cleaning results with any good soap or detergent. However, if you wash extremely heavily soiled or very large loads, you may want to add slightly more Clorox.

- Large top-loading automatic .... 1-1/2 cups
- Regular top-loading automatic .... 1 cup
- Front-loading automatic .... 1/2 cup
- Heavily soiled laundry—
  increase amount above by .... 1/4 cup
- Hand laundry—2 gallons of sudsy water .... 1/8 cup

WHAT FABRICS CAN YOU BLEACH?
Cotton, linen, synthetics, permanent press and most colored fabrics can be safely bleached. In fact, most garments that have "Do Not Bleach" care labels are actually bleach-safe. You can test any article to determine if it is bleach-safe by applying one drop of a test solution (1 tablespoon of Clorox with 1/4 cup of water) to a hidden part of the fabric. Be sure to check all colors including trim. Let stand 1 minute, then blot dry. If there is no color change the article can be safely bleached. Do not use Clorox on silk, wool, mohair, leather, spandex, or non-fast colors. Repeated use on flame-retardant fabrics made of 100% cotton may cause loss of flame retardancy.

HOW SHOULD YOU ADD CLOROX TO YOUR WASHLOAD?
Select the way to add Clorox that is easiest for you: in the wash water before the laundry is put in, or diluted with a quart of water after the washer has begun agitating. For a washer with automatic bleach dispenser, follow the manufacturer's instructions.

WHAT SPECIAL LAUNDRY PROBLEMS CAN CLOROX HELP SOLVE?
Diapers, baby clothes, and children's bed-covers can be cleaned by following the regular Clorox laundry instructions. Washing with Clorox will remove stains, eliminate most germs, and tend to reduce diaper irritation. However, repeated use on flame-retardant sleepwear made of 100% cotton may cause loss of flame retardancy.

Particularly tough laundry problems such as blood, berries, perspiration or other stubborn stains may require more than one washing with Clorox or soaking for 5 minutes in a solution of 1/4 cup Clorox to a gallon of cool sudsy water prior to washing with Clorox. Write for a free Clorox "Guide to Cleaner Washes" chart or other information on laundry or house cleaning to The Clorox Company, P.O. Box 24305, Oakland, CA 94623.

CAUTION: Clorox may be harmful if swallowed or may cause severe eye irritation if splashed in eyes. If swallowed, feed milk. If splashed in eyes, flood with water. Call physician. Skin irritant; if contact with skin, wash off with water. ● Do not use Clorox with ammonia or products containing acids such as toilet bowl cleaners, rust removers or vinegar. To do so will release hazardous gases. Prolonged contact with metal may cause pitting or discoloration. Do not use this bottle for storage of any other liquid but Clorox.   MANUFACTURED BY AND ©THE CLOROX COMPANY, OAKLAND, CA 94623   MADE IN U.S.A.   EPA REG. NO 5813-1

b. Immediately under the words EVERY DETERGENT NEEDS CLOROX, what three things are listed that Clorox is supposed to do?

(1) _____

(2) _____

(3) _____

c. If too little Clorox is used in a wash, what happens to the fabrics? _____

_____

_____

d. Name three of the stubborn stains that may require more than one washing with Clorox.

(1) _____

(2) _____

(3) _____

3. FINDING WARNINGS/CAUTIONS ON LABELS

There are several different kinds of cautions on some household product labels. Using information from the **Clorox** label, write the cautions for the following:

a. If Clorox is swallowed, what should one drink? _____

_____

b. If Clorox gets in a person's eyes, what should that person do? _____

_____

c. Clorox should not be used with what other products?

(1) _____

(2) _____

d. Should anything else be put in an empty Clorox bottle? _____

Why? _____

_____

e. How much Clorox should be used to clean a kitchen sink? _____

_____

From *Reading for Survival in Today's Society*, Volume One, ©1978 Goodyear Publishing Company, Inc.

f. Which caution is printed in the largest letters? _____

_____

_____

g. How much Clorox per gallon of sudsy water should be used to clean

floors? _____

_____

h. What type of floor should not be cleaned with Clorox? _____

_____

4. **READING BASIC INFORMATION ON LABELS**
   There is certain general information found on most food labels. Read the
   My*T*Fine label and answer the following questions:

   a. What is the net weight? _____

   b. What is the brand name? _____

   c. What is the flavor? _____

d. What is the food? _____

e. Does it require cooking? _____

5. COMPARING INFORMATION ON DIFFERENT LABELS

Read the information on the **My*T*Fine** label and the **Hawaiian Punch** label. Write information requested on the chart below. If one of the labels does not have the information, write "not shown" in the appropriate place on the chart.

	MY*T*FINE	HAWAIIAN PUNCH
Net weight	_____	_____
Artificial ingredients identified	_____	_____
Name of company that made the food	_____	_____
City and state where company is located	_____	_____
Name of product	_____	_____
Flavor of product	_____	_____
Number of calories	_____	_____

other ideas

A. Make a list of specialized vocabulary found on labels. Discuss why you consider these words specialized.

B. Read the ingredients on five different food can or box labels. Circle only the words you know. Ask the librarian for assistance in locating the meaning of other words, such as *sodium glutamate, monosodium glutamate,* etc.

C. Compare information contained on three different clothing labels.

D. Using only information found on a label, make up a true-false test. Exchange tests with another student, mark the answers, and then refer to the appropriate label to check your work. Examples of the kinds of questions to write are:

T   F   This shirt can be dry cleaned.
T   F   This blouse should be twisted while it is wet.
T   F   This sweater is made of man-made fabric.
T   F   The food in this can weighs six pounds.

From *Reading for Survival in Today's Society*, Volume One, ©1978 Goodyear Publishing Company, Inc.

It's Real! Fruit Punch

Hawaiian Punch is a real fruit punch with 7 real sunshine fruit juices in one delicious, refreshing drink.

SHAKE CAN • SERVE COLD

as is, or with a squeeze of lemon or lime. Keep opened can chilled.

Each 6 oz. serving contains 50% of U.S. recommended daily allowance of Vitamin C (U.S. RDA).

A PRODUCT OF U.S.A.
1.36 Liters

ENRICHED WITH VITAMIN C

HAWAIIAN PUNCH®

FRUIT JUICY RED

WITH 7 REAL FRUIT JUICES AND OTHER NATURAL FLAVORS

K

NET 46 FL. OZ. (1 QT. 14 OZ.)

"PUNCHY"

Distributed by
RJR Foods, Inc.
General Offices:
Winston-Salem, N.C.
27102

RJR Foods

NUTRITION INFORMATION PER SERVING

Serving size: 6 fl. oz.,
Servings per container   7-2/3.
Calories 90, Protein 0, Carbohydrates 22g.,
Fat 0.

Percentage of U.S. recommended daily allowance (U.S. RDA):

Vitamin C: 50%

Contains less than 2 percent of the U.S. RDA of Protein, Vitamin A, Thiamine, Riboflavin, Niacin, Calcium and Iron.

CONTAINS 11% FRUIT JUICE

CONTENTS: Water, sugar and corn syrups, fruit juices and purees (concentrated pineapple, orange and grapefruit juices; passionfruit juice, apricot, papaya and guava purees), citric acid (provides tartness), natural fruit flavors, Vitamin C, dextrin (a flavor carrier), artificial color, ethyl maltol (a flavor enhancer).

ARTIFICIALLY COLORED

0   48300 06105

E. Group labels according to topics, such as transportation, food, medicine, cleaning materials, furniture, and clothing. Collect labeled items that can be associated (even remotely) with these topics. Display and discuss their labels.

F. Survey food items in your kitchen to determine how many different states are represented on the labels. Make a list of the states you find.

G. Create a new product. Try to make something unusual and funny. Make a label for the product, place the item in a can or box, and paste the label on the container.

H. Select several common prepared food items. Examples include canned sausages, dog food, and canned stew. Prepare a list of the ingredients found in each, and on a separate sheet of paper write the names of each food product. See if someone can name the product by reading only the ingredients. Use the list of names to check the answers.

I. Survey the medicine cabinet at home. Make a list of suggestions or warnings given on labels.

J. Read the labels on cleaning products. Make a list of the antidotes recommended if the substance is swallowed, or gets in the eye or on the skin.

K. Around the edge of a paper plate or pizza disk, write common antidotes and/or warning signs. On clothespins, write the product name and/or meaning of the sign. Place the correct clothespin over the antidote or sign found on the paper plate or pizza disk.

key words & phrases

warning	synthetic	induce	permanent press
caution	precaution	prescription	dry clean only
dosage	delicate	contents	ventilation
usage	puncture	internally	dust-repellent
daily	additive	formula	preservative

From *Reading for Survival in Today's Society*, Volume One, © 1978 Goodyear Publishing Company, Inc.

self-evaluation

	date completed	possible score	your score	EXPERT	AVERAGE	FAIR	HELP!
1. Noting essential information on medicine labels		**5**					
2. Identifying different kinds of information on labels		**9**					
3. Finding warnings/cautions on labels		**10**					
4. Reading basic information on labels		**5**					
5. Comparing information on different labels		**14**					

CIRCLE **other ideas**
COMPLETED: A B C D E
F G H I J K

TOTAL POSSIBLE POINTS:
43

YOUR TOTAL POINTS:

How did you rate yourself?

name & date

printed
directions

2

PRINTED DIRECTIONS

A surprising number of products have corresponding printed directions. Off/on switches on lamps and stoves, recipes on food cans, directions for assembling a bicycle, and instructions for cleaning clothes are only a few of the different kinds of printed directions people may encounter. There are specific directions for understanding some processes, such as the development of mold, the growth of plants, and the detection of atmospheric conditions. *Without the ability to interpret printed directions, a person is severely handicapped and must rely on personal judgment or oral directions from another person.* Lessons to help students learn not only to identify different kinds of directions from a multitude of sources but also to read the directions both literally and critically should be planned.

Specific reading lessons emphasized in this module are: (1) following directions to make a liquid food; (2) following directions to make a main-dish meal; (3) following directions to complete application forms; (4) following directions to complete parts of a federal income tax form; and (5) following directions from notes written by someone else.

materials

Students should collect and bring to class any kind of written or printed directions. Examples include instructions for building an object, completing a form, following a process, or playing a game.

survival reading skills

1. FOLLOWING DIRECTIONS TO MAKE A LIQUID FOOD

Read the **Hawaiian Punch** label and answer the following:

a. Into what kind of container should you mix the drink?_____

_____

b. What liquid should you add to the mix? _____

c. How many scoops of Hawaiian Punch Drink Mix do you use to make

4 servings?_____

1 gallon?_____

1 serving?_____

2 quarts? _____

d. If you use all the drink mix, how many quarts will you make?_____

_____

2. FOLLOWING DIRECTIONS TO MAKE A MAIN-DISH MEAL

Read the directions on the **Chun King** label and answer the following questions:

a. In making the sauce, which do you do *first*, cook over medium heat or

add water?_____

b. In making the patties, which do you do *first*, add the vegetables or beat

the eggs?_____

_____

c. To cook the patties, you need _____ tablespoons of oil and

_____ cup egg mixture.

d. Are eggs in the mix or do you supply the eggs? _____

_____

From *Reading for Survival in Today's Society*, Volume One, © 1978 Goodyear Publishing Company, Inc.

REPLACE PLASTIC LID TIGHTLY AFTER USE. KEEP IN COOL, DRY PLACE.

DIRECTIONS: To make the amounts listed below—Pour Hawaiian Punch drink mix into non-metal container, add water, stir—Serve chilled.

TO MAKE	MEASURE HAWAIIAN PUNCH DRINK MIX	WITH THIS MUCH WATER
1 Serving (8 fl. oz.)	½ Scoop (2 tablespoons)	1 cup (8 oz.)
4 Servings (1 quart)	2 Scoops (½ cup or 8 tablespoons)	1 quart (4 cups)
8 servings (2 quarts)	4 Scoops	2 quarts
16 servings (1 gallon)	8 Scoops	1 gallon (4 quarts)

NUTRITION INFORMATION PER SERVING

SERVING SIZE: 8 FL. OZ.
SERVINGS PER CONTAINER: 32
CALORIES 100, PROTEIN 0, CARBOHYDRATES 25g, FAT 0.

PERCENTAGE OF U.S. RECOMMENDED
DAILY ALLOWANCES (U.S. RDA)

VITAMIN C   50%
CONTAINS LESS THAN 2% OF THE U.S. RDA OF PROTEIN, VITAMIN A, THIAMINE, RIBOFLAVIN, NIACIN, CALCIUM AND IRON.

INGREDIENTS: SUGAR, DEXTROSE, CITRIC ACID (PROVIDES TARTNESS), NATURAL AND ARTIFICIAL FLAVORS, SODIUM CITRATE (REGULATES TARTNESS), TRICALCIUM PHOSPHATE (PREVENTS CAKING), VITAMIN C, CELLULOSE GUM (ADDS BODY), ARTIFICIAL COLOR.

RJR Foods DIST. BY RJR FOODS, INC.,
WINSTON-SALEM, N.C. 27102   807.9 g

0 48300 06203

HAWAIIAN PUNCH DRINK MIX
CONTAINS NO FRUIT JUICE

STRAWBERRY PUNCH
ARTIFICIALLY FLAVORED

VITAMIN C ENRICHED

MAKES 8 QTS.
PRE-SWEETENED

FREE SCOOP INSIDE

NET WT. 28½ OZ. (1 LB. 12½ OZ.)

From Reading for Survival in Today's Society, Volume One, ©1978 Goodyear Publishing Company, Inc.

CHUN KING — FOR DELICIOUS MEALS YOUR FAMILY WILL REMEMBER

EGG FOO YUNG, often called the Chinese omelet, is a delicious light meal, nice for brunch, lunch or supper. You beat your own fresh eggs, with a delectable seasoning mix, add the well drained Oriental vegetables and fry in patties. A pleasant sauce adds a mouthwatering touch. Children love miniature Egg Foo Yung patties.

BASIC DIRECTIONS

SAUCE: In a saucepan, combine 1½ cups cold water and contents of SAUCE mix packet. Cook over medium heat, stirring constantly, until sauce begins to thicken. Keep warm while preparing patties.

PATTIES: Beat 4 eggs with a fork. Add thoroughly drained vegetables and then the PATTIE seasoning mix. Mix well.

TO COOK PATTIES: Heat 2 table-spoons oil in a skillet. Ladle in ⅓ cup egg mixture, spreading vegetables evenly. Cook patties over medium heat, until brown on one side. Turn carefully and brown other side.

Makes six 5-inch patties.

SERVE WITH WARM SAUCE

FOR MORE MEALS WITH ORIENTAL FLAIR THAT YOUR FAMILY WILL REMEMBER, TRY THESE AND OTHER EASY-TO-PREPARE CHUN KING PRODUCTS:

- Chinatown-Style Frozen Dinners
- Pepper Oriental Divider-Pak
- Other Stir-Fry Entrees
- Chow Mein Noodles and Soy Sauce
- Orient Express Frozen Dinners
- Chicken Chow Mein Divider-Pak
- Frozen Entrees Including Chicken Chow Mein and Sweet & Sour Pork
- Frozen Egg Rolls

TRY VARIATIONS ON SIDE PANEL

---

3. FOLLOWING DIRECTIONS TO COMPLETE APPLICATION FORMS

Locate the following parts of the **Allstate Life Insurance Company** form and write only the directions given.

a. In item 1, two directions are given concerning how to write your name. What are these two directions?

(1) _____

(2) _____
_____

b. In item 3, a direction is given concerning the number of years a person has lived at the present address. How many years? _____

From Reading for Survival in Today's Society, Volume One, ©1978 Goodyear Publishing Company, Inc.

c. In item 6, there is another direction about years. What is it? _____

_____

_____

_____

d. In item 16a, what direction is given if you answer yes?_____

_____

_____

e. In item 19, what five items are you supposed to give if you answer yes?

(1) _____

(2) _____

(3) _____

(4) _____

(5) _____

4. FOLLOWING DIRECTIONS TO COMPLETE PARTS OF A FEDERAL INCOME TAX FORM

Use the following information to complete the appropriate spaces on the **1040A** form:
- You are married and are filing a joint return.
- You have two dependent children.
- Your total income (wages) for the year is $12,458.90.

Use your present address to complete spaces A, B, and C. You may "invent" any other information that is required, such as your occupation and/or social security number.

5. FOLLOWING DIRECTIONS FROM NOTES WRITTEN BY SOMEONE ELSE

Work with a partner. Each of you should write directions for traveling from one place to another place within the classroom or school. Exchange papers and follow the directions, actually traveling the described route. Afterward, discuss the directions with your partner. Which parts were clear and correct? Which parts were misleading or incorrect?

From Reading for Survival in Today's Society, Volume One. ©1978 Goodyear Publishing Company, Inc.

Part I—Application For Life Insurance

"Insured" means Annuitant if an Annuity policy is applied for.

ALLSTATE LIFE INSURANCE COMPANY
(Herein called Allstate)

NO. L 640707

—From Reading for Survival in Today's Society, Volume One, ©1978 Goodyear Publishing Company, Inc.

---

1. PROPOSED INSURED (Please Print)   ☐ MALE   ☐ FEMALE

First Name   Initial   Last Name

☐ Single ☐ Married ☐ Divorced ☐ Separated ☐ Widowed

2. PRESENT ADDRESS—   How long?

Number   Street

City and State   County   Zip Code   Area Tel.

3. PRIOR ADDRESS—Complete if at present address less than 2 yrs.

4. OCCUPATION—Job Title

5. EMPLOYER'S NAME   How long?

BUSINESS ADDRESS—

Number   Street

City   State   Zip Code

6. PRIOR EMPLOYER'S NAME—Complete if changed within 2 years.

ADDRESS

7. a. BIRTH DATE MO. / DAY / YR.   **b. INS. AGE**   **c. BIRTH PLACE**

8. a. FACE AMOUNT $ **b. PLAN OF INSURANCE**
(Exclude Rider Amount)   (Mortgage Prot.-Yrs. ☐10 ☐15 ☐20 ☐25 ☐30)

9. If available, is automatic premium loan requested? ☐ YES ☐ NO

10. a. ADDITIONAL BENEFITS — Check each one desired.
☐ Waiver of Premium.   ☐ Accidental Death Benefit.
☐ Family Income on Proposed Insured _____ units for _____ yrs.
☐ Accidental Death Benefit on Proposed Insured's Family Income Rider
☐ Future Purchase Privilege.   ☐ Disability Income $_____ mo.
☐ Family Plan Rider _____ units.   ☐ Annuity Purchase Option.
☐ Payor Benefit on Owner.
b. ADDITIONAL BENEFITS — Available With Family Plans Only.
☐ Additional Accidental Death Benefit on ☐ Insured ☐ Spouse
☐ Family Income on Spouse _____ units for _____ years.
☐ Accidental Death Benefit on Spouse's Family Income Rider.

11. PAYMENT PLAN ☐ Monthly ☐ Quarterly ☐ Semi-Annual ☐ Annual
☐ Check Plan — attach LB7.
☐ Payroll Deduction — attach authorization

12. SEND PREMIUM NOTICES TO:
Proposed Insured's: ☐ Residence ☐ Business Address
☐ Owner's Address ☐ Other—(enter in Remarks below)

13. Were you informed that a medical examination is required of:
Proposed Insured? ☐ Yes ☐ No   Spouse? ☐ Yes ☐ No

REMARKS

---

14. BENEFICIARY

FOR ALL PLANS EXCEPT FAMILY PLANS a. PRIMARY if living,

First Name   Initial   Last Name   Relationship

b. CONTINGENT if living,

First Name   Initial   Last Name   Relationship

FOR FAMILY PLANS ONLY
Unless indicated otherwise in Remarks below,
☐ TWO PARENT — Beneficiary is the Proposed Insured, if living;
Otherwise the Spouse, if living; Otherwise, the living lawful children
and stepchildren of the insured, equally,
☐ ONE PARENT — Beneficiary is the Proposed Insured, if living;
Otherwise,

c.   First Name   Initial   Last Name   Relationship
if living; Otherwise the living lawful children and stepchildren of the
Insured, equally.

15. OWNER — Proposed Insured (unless otherwise named below).
a.

b. ADDRESS: ☐ Same as Proposed Insured, OR —   First Name   Initial   Last Name   Relationship

Number   Street

City   State   Zip Code

c. CONTINGENT OWNER —

First Name   Initial   Last Name   Relationship

16. In the PAST 3 YEARS, has Proposed Insured: YES NO
a. had a driver's license suspended or revoked, been charged
with 3 or more moving traffic violations, or had 2 or more
accidents while operating a motor vehicle? .... ☐   ☐
If "YES", give driver license number and state.
Lic. No. _____ State. _____
b. flown other than as a scheduled airline passenger, or intend
to engage in any such flying in the NEXT 12 MONTHS? ☐   ☐
c. engaged in any racing, parachuting or scuba diving activities, or intend to engage in any such activities in the NEXT
12 MONTHS? ☐   ☐
d. resided outside of the U.S. or Canada or contemplated
such residence in the NEXT 12 MONTHS? .... ☐   ☐
If "YES", Complete applicable Supplemental Questionnaire.

17. LIST LIFE & A D B INSURANCE ON PROPOSED INSURED - Check if none ☐

Company Name and State	Date Issued	Amount Ins.	A.D.B.

18. Has any person proposed for insurance in No. 1 and 20:   YES NO
a. applied for Life or Health insurance, or reinstatement
thereof, in PAST 3 YEARS, without receiving it exactly as
requested? ☐   ☐
b. any application for life insurance pending in this or any
other company? ☐   ☐

19. Will life insurance or an annuity with any company be replaced
or changed by the insurance requested on this application? ☐   ☐
*If "YES" in question 18 or 19, give person and company names,
insurance amount, date, and reason for "YES" in Remarks.*

Short Form 1040A   U.S. Individual Income Tax Return

Department of the Treasury
Internal Revenue Service   **1975**

Please print or type

Name (If joint return, give first names and initials of both) — **Last name**

Present home address (Number and street, including apartment number, or rural route)

City, town or post office, State and ZIP code

Your social security number

Spouse's social security no.

Occupation — Yours ▲ / Spouse's ▲

For Privacy Act Notification, see page 2 of Instructions.

For IRS use only

Requested by Census Bureau for Revenue Sharing

A In what city, town, village, etc., do you live?

B Do you live within the legal limits of the city, town, etc.? ☐ Yes ☐ No ☐ Don't know

C In what county and State do you live? County / State

D In what township do you live? (See page 5.)

Filing Status (check only ONE box)

1 ☐ Single
2 ☐ Married filing joint return (even if only one had income)
3 ☐ Married filing separately. If spouse is also filing give spouse's social security number in designated space above and enter full name here ▲
4 ☐ Unmarried Head of Household (See page 4 of Instructions)
5 ☐ Qualifying widow(er) with dependent child (Year spouse died ▲ 19). See page 4 of Instructions.

Exemptions

6a Regular ☐ Yourself ☐ Spouse — Enter number of boxes checked ▲
b First names of your dependent children who lived with you ____ — Enter number ▲
c Number of other dependents (from line 22) ▲
d Total (add lines 6a, b, and c) — Enter number of boxes checked ▲
e Age 65 or over . ☐ Yourself ☐ Spouse / Blind ☐ Yourself ☐ Spouse — Enter number of boxes checked ▲
7 Total (add lines 6d and e) ▲

8 Presidential Election Campaign Fund . ▲ Do you wish to designate $1 of your taxes for this fund? ☐ Yes ☐ No — Note: If you check the "Yes" box(es) it will not increase your tax or reduce your refund.
If joint return, does your spouse wish to designate $1? ☐ Yes ☐ No

Attach Copy B of Forms W-2 and Check or Money Order here

9 Wages, salaries, tips, and other employee compensation (Attach Forms W-2. If unavailable, see page 6 of Instructions.) | 9
10a Dividends (if over $400, see Instructions at top of page 3) $ .... 10b Less exclusion $ .... Balance ▲ | 10c
11 Interest income (if over $400, see Instructions at top of page 3) | 11
12 Total (add lines 9, 10c, and 11) (Adjusted Gross Income) | 12

● If you want IRS to figure your tax, see page 6 of Instructions.
● If line 12 is under $15,000, find tax in Tax Tables (on pages 8–18) and enter on line 13a, on the back.
● If line 12 is $15,000 or more, figure your tax using the Tax Computation Worksheet on page 18 of Instructions.

(If less than $8,000, see page 18 of Instructions on "Earned Income Credit.")

other ideas

A. Draw a design using only geometric shapes. Write directions for making the design. Give the directions, but not the design, to another student, who must recreate the design from the written directions only. When the second design is complete, compare it with the original design. Discuss how the directions might be changed to make the task easier.

B. Compare at least three different forms, noting the item that is supposed to be completed first on each.

C. When reading basic assembly diagrams, note the numbered sequence of steps and corresponding numbered sequential figures. Either pantomime the construction, using similar objects in the room, or use a small scale model to visualize the procedure.

D. Complete a model kit in class by following assembly/construction directions.

E. Look at a picture of any geometric shape, such as a cube or triangle. Without showing the picture or telling what it is, describe it to a partner or other members of the class, who must attempt to draw it from your description. Compare the finished drawings with the original geometric shape. Were your directions clear? How could you improve them?

F. Forms are revised frequently. Ask the nearest Internal Revenue Office for copies of the latest 1040 form. Is the information on it the same as that on the 1040A form in this book? If not, what changes have been made?

key words & phrases

add	prior	take	moisten
timed	complete	seal	capsule
combine	remarks	adhere	point
print	sign	follow	enlarge
present	release	empty	enumerate

self-evaluation

	date completed	possible score	your score	EXPERT	AVERAGE	FAIR	HELP!
1. Following directions to make a liquid food		7					
2. Following directions to make a main-dish meal		5					
3. Following directions to complete application forms		10					
4. Following directions to complete parts of a federal income tax form		25					
5. Following directions from notes written by someone else		1					

CIRCLE **other ideas**
COMPLETED: A B C D E F

TOTAL POSSIBLE POINTS:
48

YOUR TOTAL POINTS:

How did you rate yourself?

schedules

3

3

SCHEDULES

In addition to the unwritten daily schedule each of us follows with different degrees of variation, there are many printed schedules that affect various aspects of our lives. Most recreational areas—parks, theaters, stadiums—have printed schedules that must be read and followed. Special events are scheduled, and our arriving on time may depend on our reading the schedule correctly. Perhaps the most surprising fact concerning schedules is the large increase in the number of persons who read airline timetables: *In 1950, 19 million persons traveled by air; in 1974, 207 million read airline schedules and got on and off airplanes.*[1]

Specific reading lessons emphasized in this module are: (1) reading airline time schedules; (2) reading symbols on airline schedules; (3) locating information about airline travel; (4) finding information about cost of airline flights; and (5) identifying scheduled events in newspapers.

materials

Students should bring to class copies of athletic and theater programs; television guides of various kinds; camp agendas; bus, airline, train, and other public conveyance timetables; school calendars; and other printed schedules.

[1]United States Bureau of the Census, *Statistical Abstract of the United States: 1975* (96th ed.; Washington, D.C.: U.S. Bureau of the Census, 1975), p. 592.

survival reading skills

1. READING AIRLINE TIME SCHEDULES
Read the **United Airlines** schedule and complete the following:

a. If you leave Miami, Florida, at 9:40 A.M. and fly to Pittsburgh, Pennsylvania, you would arrive at what time?_____

b. If you leave Milwaukee, Wisconsin, at 5:25 P.M. and fly to Bakersfield, California, you would arrive at what time? _____

c. If you leave Milwaukee, Wisconsin, at 11:45 A.M. and fly to Honolulu, Hawaii, you would arrive at what time?_____

d. Which takes the longest flight time, the 11:15 A.M. flight from Miami to Seattle/Tacoma, Washington, or the 11:45 A.M. flight from Milwaukee to Bakersfield, California? _____

_____

_____

e. How many flights are there each day from Milwaukee to Fresno, California? _____

f. How long does it take to fly from Milwaukee to Atlanta if you leave at 7:11 A.M.?_____

_____

If you leave Milwaukee at 3:10 P.M.? _____

_____

2. READING SYMBOLS ON AIRLINE SCHEDULES
Use both the **United Airlines** schedule and the **Decoding of Reference Marks** information to answer the following:

a. Which flight has movies, the one to Honolulu or the one to Denver?

_____

From Reading for Survival in Today's Society, Volume One, ©1978 Goodyear Publishing Company, Inc.

⫴ UNITED AIRLINES   Eff. 3/2/76

Leave	Arrive	Flight	Service Via

Miami, Fla. (EST)
Fort Lauderdale/Hollywood

To New York, N.Y.
Newark, N.J. (EST)
Leave	Arrive	Flight	Service Via
G 1:30p(M)	5:30p(L)	268	▼✗ 1
G 1:30p(F)	5:30p(L)	906/268	▼✗ Pit

To Norfolk/Portsmouth,
Virginia Beach Va. (EST)
8:30a(F)	12:12p	836/802	▼✗ Atl
2:28p(M)	6:02p	570/401	▼✗ Atl
2:29p(F)	6:02p	956/401	▼✗ Atl

To Philadelphia, Penn. (EST)
| G 3:00p(M) | 7:22p | 968 | ▼➡ 1 |

To Pittsburgh, Penn. (EST)
9:40a(F)	12:05p	964	▼✗ 0
1:30p(M)	3:57p	268	▼✗ 0
1:30p(F)	3:58p	906	▼✗ 0
5:00p(M)	7:29p	578	▼✗● 0
▮ 10:00p(M)	12:27a	1228	▼ 0

To Raleigh/
Durham N.C. (EST)
| 8:30a(F) | 12:50p | 836/824 | ▼✗ Atl |

To Rochester, N.Y. (EST)
8:30a(F)	1:42p	836	▼✗ 2
2:29p(F)	7:00p	956	▼✗ 1
3:00p(M)	5:50p	968	▼➡ 0
5:45p(F)	9:22p	972	▼✗ 1
▮ 10:00p(M)	2:27a	1228	▼✗ 2

To Saginaw/Midland/Bay City,
Mich. (EST)
| 4:00p(M) | 8:42p | 576/396 | ▼✗● Cle |
| 4:15p(F) | 8:42p | 692/396 | ▼✗● Cle |

To Seattle/
Tacoma, Wash. (PST)
| 11:00a(M) | 5:55p | 982/155 | ♪▼✗● Cle |
| 11:15a(M) | 5:55p | 568/155 | ♪▼✗● Cle |

To South Bend, Ind. (EST)
G 4:00p(M)	8:32p	576/421	▼✗● Cle
P 4:00p(M)	9:21p	576/969	▼✗● Cle
G 4:15p(F)	8:32p	692/421	▼✗ Cle
P 4:15p(F)	9:21p	692/969	▼✗ Cle

To Toledo, O. (EST)
G 11:00a(M)	3:23p	982/779	▼✗ Cle
G 11:15a(M)	3:23p	568/779	▼✗ Cle
4:00p(M)	8:10p	576/357	▼✗● Cle
4:15p(F)	8:10p	692/357	▼✗● Cle

To Washington D.C./
Baltimore, Md. (EST)
| G 8:30a(F) | 3:02p(I) | 836 | ▼✗ 3 |

To Youngstown/Warren/, O.
Sharon, Penn. (EST)
G 1:30p(F)	5:37p	906/672	▼✗ Pit
G 1:30p(M)	5:37p	268/672	▼✗ Pit
5:00p(M)	8:45p	578/699	▼✗● Pit

Midland,. Mich.
SEE Saginaw, Mich. Listing

Milwaukee, Wisc. (CST)   273-8400

To Atlanta, Ga. (EST)
| 7:11a | 11:32a | 852/269 | ▼✗ Cle |
| 3:10p | 7:43p | 306/475 | ▼✗● Cle |

To Bakersfield, Cal. (PST)
9:40a	1:33p	733/854	♪▼✗ Lax
10:30a	3:41p	499/721	▼✗ SFO
11:45a	4:38p	701/864	♪▼✗ Lax
▮ 5:25p	10:02p	241/894	♪▼✗● Lax

To Baltimore, Md. (EST)
7:11a	10:58a	852/966	✗ Cle
1 G 3:10p	7:38p	306/714	▼➡ Cle
4 3:10p	7:38p	306/714	▼➡ Cle

To Boise, Id. (MST)
| 8:10a | 12:30p | 243/621 | ♪▼✗ Den |
| 5:25p | 9:45p | 241/311 | ♪▼✗● Den |

To Boston, Mass. (EST)
| 7:11a | 11:18a | 852/732 | ✗ Cle |
| 3:10p | 7:38p | 306 | ▼➡ 1 |

To Charleston, W.V. (EST)
| 3:10p | 6:59p | 306/839 | ▼ Cle |

To Cleveland, O. (EST)
| 7:11a | 9:15a | 852 | ✗ 0 |
| 3:10p | 5:12p | 306 | ▼ 0 |

To Denver, Colo. (MST)
1 P 7:50a	9:11a	1439	♪▼✗ 0
8:10a	9:31a	243	♪▼✗ 0
11:45a	1:06p	701	♪▼✗ 0
5:25p	6:46p	241	♪▼✗● 0

To Fresno, Cal. (PST)
9:40a	1:33p	733/554	♪▼✗ Lax
11:45a	4:45p	701/288	♪▼✗ Lax
5:25p	10:01p	241/461	♪▼✗● Den

To Grand Jct. Colo. (MST)
3 R 11:45a	2:40p	701/1419	♪▼✗ Den
2 11:45a	2:45p	701/857	♪▼✗ Den
3 11:45a	3:10p	701/857	♪▼✗ Den

To Hartford, Conn.
Springfield, Mass. (EST)
| 7:11a | 11:21a | 852 | ✗ 1 |

To Hilo, Hi. (HST)
| R 10:30a | 4:40p | 499/187 | ☙▼✗ SFO |

To Honolulu, Hi. (HST)
9:40a	4:35p(H)	733/193	☙▼✗★ Lax
R 10:30a	4:40p(I)	499/187	☙▼✗★ SFO
10:30a	5:05p(H)	499/97	☙▼✗★ SFO
11:45a	7:35p(H)	701/5	▼✗★ Lax

To Jacksonville, Fla. (EST)
| 7:11a | 1:25p | 852/269 | ▼✗ Cle |

To Las Vegas, Nev. (PST)
R 8:10a	10:36a	243/753	♪▼✗ Den
8:10a	11:33a	243/249	♪▼✗ Den
4 D 8:50a	10:30a	555	♪▼✗ 0
1 R 8:50a	10:30a	555	♪▼✗ 0
11:45a	2:38p	701/855	♪▼✗ Den
5:25p	8:48p	241/305	♪▼✗● Den

To Los Angeles, /
Ontario, Cal. (PST)
9:40a	11:45a(L)	733	♪▼✗ 0
10:30a	3:04p(L)	499/903	♪▼✗ SFO
11:45a	3:05p(O)	701/639	♪▼✗ Den
11:45a	3:05p(L)	701	♪▼✗ 1
5:25p	8:57p(L)	241	♪▼✗● 1

To Merced, Cal. (PST)
| 10:30a | 2:48p | 499/829 | ▼✗ SFO |

To Miami, Fla. (EST)
Fort Lauderdale/Hollywood
7:11a	12:25p(F)	852/967	▼✗ Cle
7:11a	12:35p(M)	852/595	▼✗● Cle
3:10p	8:35p(F)	306/333	▼✗ Cle
3:10p	8:50p(M)	306/579	▼✗ Cle
▮ G 8:10p	1:37a(M)	588/1227	▼ Pit

To Monterey, Cal. (PST)
| 10:30a | 2:44p | 499/895 | ▼✗ SFO |
| 11:45a | 4:59p | 701/342 | ♪▼✗ Lax |

To New York, N.Y.
Newark, N.J. (EST)
7:11a	11:06a(L)	852/840	✗ Cle
7:11a	11:15a(E)	852/572	✗ Cle
3:10p	7:14p(E)	306/72	▼➡ Cle
3:10p	7:23p(L)	306/394	▼➡ Cle
3:10p	7:35p(J)	306/422	▼➡ Cle

To Pendleton, Ore. (PST)
| 8:10a | 2:09p | 243/161/375 | ♪▼✗ Den /Sc |

To Philadelphia, Penn. (EST)
| 7:11a | 11:03a | 852/406 | ✗ Cle |
| G 3:10p | 7:22p | 306/940 | ▼➡ Cle |

To Pittsburgh, Penn. (EST)
3:10p	6:43p	306/464	▼ Cle
1 P 6:35p	8:47p	1420	▼ 0
1 N 7:05p	9:17p	950	▼ 0
4 G 8:10p	10:22p	588	▼ 0
1 R 8:10p	10:22p	588	▼ 0

To Portland, Ore. (PST)
8:10a	12:22p	243/811	♪▼✗ Den
11:45a	3:35p	701/743	♪▼✗ Den
5:25p	9:30p	241/167	♪▼✗● Den

To Providence, R.I. (EST)
| G 3:10p | 7:21p | 306/720 | ▼➡ Cle |

On April 26, Daylight Savings Time becomes effective in all states except Indiana and the Hawaiian Islands. Consult United or your travel agent for schedule adjustments after April 24 in these states.

From *Reading for Survival in Today's Society*, Volume One, ©1978 Goodyear Publishing Company, Inc.

b. Which flight has a meal, the one to Hartford or the one to Charleston, West Virginia? _____

_____

c. Which three flights are *not* available on Fridays from Miami to Rochester, New York?

(1) _____

(2) _____

(3) _____

d. Which flight does *not* have audio (music) in flight, the one from Miami to Pittsburgh, or the one from Milwaukee to Portland? _____

_____

e. If you see a flight marked *Q*, what does the *Q* mean? _____

_____

f. Find one flight that becomes effective on April 12. Write the time that flight leaves and arrives. _____

_____

```
Decoding Of Reference Marks:
  A—Except Sunday         F—Except Friday          L—Wednesday only
  B—Except Monday         G—Except Saturday        M—Thursday only
  C—Except Tuesday        H—Except Sat. & Sun.     N—Friday only
  D—Except Wednesday      I—Sunday only            P—Saturday only
  E—Except Thursday       J—Monday only            Q—Sat. & Sun. only
                          K—Tuesday only
  R—Subject to frequency change—consult United or your travel agent for details.
  (D)—Dulles (Wash. D.C.)  (J)—Kennedy (New York)   (M)—Midway (Chi)
  (E)—Newark                   or San Jose (Calif.)      or Miami Int'l
  (F)—Ft. Lauderdale       (K)—Oakland Int'l        (N)—National (Wash. D.C.)
  (H)—Honolulu Int'l       (L)—LaGuardia (New York) (O)—O'Hare Int'l (Chi.)
  (I)—Balt/Wash. Int'l         or Los Angeles Int'l      or Ontario (Calif)
      or Hilo, Hawaii                               (S)—San Francisco Int'l

  X Meal    Snacks    Y Cocktails   Movies    Audio
  1—disc. 4/1    3—disc. 4/6    5—disc. 4/8    7—disc. 3/26
  2—eff. 4/6     4—eff. 4/1     6—eff. 4/8     8—eff. 4/12
  10—eff. 3/26
  ★—B-747 Jet            ●—DC-10 Jet
  ◆—Connection from B-747 to DC-10
  ▲—Connection from DC-10 to B-747
  Flight times and numbers shown in bold type operate in wide body jets.
```

3. LOCATING INFORMATION ABOUT AIRLINE TRAVEL

Using the **General Passenger Information**, answer the following:

a. How many pieces of baggage can you carry on board? _____

Where must you place the baggage?_____

_____

_____

b. How much does it cost to take your bicycle? _____

_____

c. Name two permitted electronic devices that are related to medical conditions.

(1) _____

(2) _____

d. Name three credit cards United will accept.

(1) _____

(2) _____

(3) _____

e. What must you have on your baggage tag? _____

_____

f. If your bag is lost in the United States, what is the greatest amount the airline will pay unless you take out extra insurance?_____

_____

g. Name four items you cannot pack in your baggage.

(1) _____

(2) _____

(3) _____

(4) _____

UNITED AIRLINES Inc.—P. O. Box 66100, CHICAGO, ILL. 60666
EXECUTIVE OFFICES Tel. 952-4000 — Cable Address, UALAIR

General Passenger Information

Agriculture Inspection, Hawaii-Mainland   Admissibility of plant products to the Mainland from Hawaii should be determined prior to check-in. Such products and baggage are subject to pre-departure agriculture inspection at the Honolulu and Hilo Airports. Please have baggage ready for examination as requested. For detailed information phone: Plant Protection and Quarantine, APHIS, USDA, Honolulu 841-3661 or 841-4342; Hilo 935-1049.

Alcoholic Beverages   Federal Aviation Agency regulations provide that no person may drink alcoholic beverages aboard an aircraft unless they have been served by the airline and no airline may serve such beverages to any person who appears to be intoxicated.

Baggage Allowance   (Per passenger) 1 piece of baggage with linear dimensions (length + height + width) not exceeding 62 inches, plus 1 piece of baggage with linear dimensions not exceeding 55 inches. One or more additional pieces, totaling no more than 45 inches may be carried on board provided it fits beneath the seat or in an approved carry-on compartment. Approximate dimensions not to exceed 9 x 13 x 23. In addition to size, each piece must not exceed 70 pounds. 66 pounds at First Class fare and 44 pounds at Coach fare for trips between the Continental U. S. and Alaska or foreign points other than Canada.

A standard fee of $5.00 for each excess or oversize piece of baggage will be charged, except for the special items listed below. These special items will always be subject to the charges listed **regardless** of the total baggage carried.

Bicycles—$10.00	Surfboards—$10.00
Scuba gear—$5.00 per set	Household pets—$15.00 per container

Baggage Liability   Baggage should be clearly tagged with your name and address. Liability for baggage for trips between points in the U.S. will not exceed $500.00 per ticket unless you declare a higher valuation and pay a slight extra charge. Excess valuation cannot be declared for certain checked valuable items such as jewelry, negotiable instruments, currency and antiques. For international trips, United's liability will not exceed $9.07 per pound for checked baggage and $400 per passenger for unchecked baggage unless you declare a higher value and pay an extra charge.

Checked Baggage   Car keys, pills, critical medicine or other items necessary for your health or well-being should remain in carry-on luggage whenever possible, as baggage, checked prior to departure, is generally unavailable again until claimed at your destination.

Class of Service   On United, you can fly First Class, Coach, or — on certain routes — Economy. First Class gives you spacious seating comfort and — time permitting — our most luxurious personalized service: complimentary cocktails, gourmet dining, and a variety of other amenities. Coach seating is comfortable but more compact and meals are hot, delicious, satisfying. Economy offers the same comfortable seating as Coach, without meals and including coffee, tea and soft drinks. Liquors, wines, etc. are available at a nominal charge in both Coach and Economy. All these services include the friendly hospitality of United's dedicated employees.

Credit Cards   You can easily arrange credit with our Personal Credit Card Plan. United also accepts American Express, Bankamericard, Carte Blanche, Diners Club, Empire, Interbank, Mastercharge, Walker Bankard and Universal Air Travel cards. Consult United or your travel agent for details.

Denied Boarding Compensation Plan   Compensation will be paid if the flight for which you have a confirmed reservation is unable to accommodate you and departs without you. Subject to the exceptions prescribed in the tariff on file, compensation will be in amounts from $25.00 to $200.00 depending upon the ticket value.

Electronic Devices   Federal Aviation regulations prohibit in flight operation of electronic devices other than portable voice recorders or electronic calculators, electric watches, hearing aids, heart pacemakers and electric shavers. Other electronic devices (including AM and FM broadcast receivers) may interfere with the navigation or communications systems of the aircraft.

Responsibility for Departures, Arrivals, Connections   United Airlines will not be responsible for damages resulting from the failure to depart or arrive at times stated in this timetable, nor for errors herein, nor for failure to make connections with planes of other lines or of this Company. Schedules subject to change without notice. Safety is our primary consideration. Schedule times published include allowances for variations in wind direction and velocity, planned ground movement of the aircraft between runway and gates and similar factors to assure gate arrivals within 15 minutes of published schedule more than 75% on the time. Schedules do not allow for abnormal air traffic and ground delays which cannot be forecast in advance.

Restricted Articles   Acid, matches, lighter fluid and hazardous articles **MUST NOT BE PACKED IN BAGGAGE.**

On April 25, Daylight Savings Time becomes effective in all states except Indiana and the Hawaiian Islands. Consult United or your travel agent for schedule adjustments after April 24 in these states.

---

4. FINDING INFORMATION ABOUT THE COST OF AIRLINE FLIGHTS

Use the **first class fare chart** to answer the following questions:

a. What is the cost of a flight from

Denver to New York/Newark?_____

Omaha to San Diego? _____

Boston to Salt Lake City?_____

Washington, D.C., to Atlanta?_____

b. If you wanted to fly from Atlanta to New York, and then from New York to Detroit, and then from Detroit to Pittsburgh, and from Pittsburgh back to Atlanta, how much would the total cost of your tickets be? Use the steps below to compute the answer.

(1) Cost from Atlanta to New York?_____

(2) Cost from New York to Detroit?_____

(3) Cost from Detroit to Pittsburgh? _____

(4) Cost from Pittsburgh to Atlanta?_____

Add the costs of all four tickets.

The total cost of your flight is _____

TYPICAL UNITED AIRLINES ONE WAY FARES   Fares included herein are not guaranteed and are subject to change without notice.

First Class Fares	ATLANTA	BOSTON	CHICAGO	CLEVELAND	DENVER	DETROIT	HONOLULU	LAS VEGAS	LOS ANGELES	MIAMI	MINNEAPOLIS/ST. PAUL	NEW YORK/NEWARK	NORFOLK/PORTSMOUTH	OMAHA	PHILADELPHIA	PITTSBURGH	PORTLAND	SALT LAKE CITY	SAN DIEGO	SAN FRANCISCO	SEATTLE/TACOMA	WASHINGTON, D.C.
ATLANTA	–	–	–	86.00		90.00				90.00		105.00	83.00	–	–	84.00	–	–	–	–	–	86.00
BOSTON	–	–	116.00	87.00	200.00		426.34	255.00	276.00	–	140.00			154.00	–		276.00	230.00	276.00	276.00	276.00	–
CHICAGO	–	116.00	–	59.00		49.00	352.86	176.00	124.00		62.00	102.00	99.00	72.00	97.00	70.00	119.00	153.00	200.00	200.00	200.00	90.00
CLEVELAND	86.00	87.00	59.00	–	148.00	33.00	380.90	206.00	227.00	136.00	92.00	70.00	73.00	102.00	65.00	34.00	227.00	181.00	227.00	227.00	227.00	58.00
DENVER	–	200.00	76.00	148.00	–	141.00	276.19	91.00	73.00			186.00	185.00	79.00	181.00	157.00	82.00	66.00	112.00	123.00	84.00	174.00
DETROIT	90.00	49.00	33.00	141.00	–		363.39	157.00	220.00		84.00	81.00	83.00	95.00	76.00	45.00	220.00	174.00	220.00	220.00	220.00	69.00
HONOLULU	–	426.34	352.86	380.90	276.19	363.39	–	230.39	204.06			417.63	415.36	332.98	411.19	388.47	204.46	275.17	204.06	204.08	204.64	404.67
LAS VEGAS	–	255.00	176.00	206.00	91.00	197.00	239.39	–	47.00			243.00	234.00	137.00	237.00	213.00	125.00	–	–	69.00	136.00	230.00
LOS ANGELES	–	276.00	124.00	227.00	73.00	220.00	204.06	47.00	–			265.00	258.00	157.00	258.00	235.00	112.00	88.00	10.15	28.00	123.00	252.00
MIAMI	90.00	–		136.00						–			109.00		129.00							
MINNEAPOLIS/ST. PAUL	–	140.00	62.00	92.00		84.00					–	130.00	132.00		126.00	102.00						122.00
NEW YORK/NEWARK	105.00	–	102.00	70.00	186.00	81.00	417.63	243.00	265.00		130.00	–		141.00	32.00		265.00	219.00	265.00	265.00	265.00	–
NORFOLK/PORTSMOUTH	83.00	–	99.00	73.00	183.00	83.00	415.36	234.00	258.00	109.00	132.00		–	140.00	45.00	60.00	86.00	217.00	258.00	258.00	266.00	37.00
OMAHA	–	154.00	72.00	102.00	79.00	95.00	332.98	137.00	157.00			141.00	140.00	–	137.00	110.00	162.00	112.00	168.00	168.00	162.00	129.00
PHILADELPHIA	–		97.00	65.00	181.00	76.00	411.19	237.00	259.00		126.00	32.00	45.00	137.00	–	60.00	259.00	214.00	259.00	259.00	259.00	
PITTSBURGH	84.00	–	70.00	34.00	157.00	45.00	388.47	213.00	235.00	129.00	102.00		60.00	110.00	60.00	–	235.00	189.00	235.00	235.00	235.00	45.00
PORTLAND	–	276.00	119.00	227.00	82.00	220.00	204.46	125.00	112.00			265.00	86.00	162.00	259.00	235.00	–	92.00	122.00	56.00	24.00	252.00
SALT LAKE CITY	–	230.00	153.00	181.00	66.00	174.00	275.17	–	88.00			219.00	217.00	112.00	214.00	189.00	92.00	–	–	90.00	98.00	207.00
SAN DIEGO	–	276.00	200.00	227.00	112.00	220.00	204.06	–	10.15			265.00	258.00	168.00	259.00	235.00	122.00	–	–	28.80	133.00	252.00
SAN FRANCISCO	–	276.00	200.00	227.00	123.00	220.00	204.08	69.00	28.00			265.00	258.00	168.00	259.00	235.00	56.00	90.00	28.80	–	98.00	252.00
SEATTLE/TACOMA	–	276.00	200.00	227.00	84.00	220.00	204.64	136.00	123.00			265.00	266.00	162.00	259.00	235.00	24.00	98.00	133.00	98.00	–	252.00
WASHINGTON, D.C.	86.00	–	90.00	58.00	174.00	69.00	404.67	230.00	252.00	–	122.00	–	37.00	129.00		45.00	252.00	207.00	252.00	252.00	252.00	–

om "Reading for Survival in Today's Society," Volume One. ©1978 Goodyear Publishing Company, Inc.

5. IDENTIFYING SCHEDULED EVENTS IN NEWSPAPERS
Refer to the **May 26, 1976, television schedule** and answer the following:

a. The 3:00 P.M. program on NBC is _____

b. The 7:00 A.M. program on ABC is _____

c. The 7:00 P.M. program on CBS is_____

d. The channel number for station KDFW is_____

e. If you watched the first 10 minutes of "Young and the Restless" on CBS

and changed to NBC, what would you then be watching?_____

_____

f. Write the name of a program you think each of the following would like:

(1) A three-year-old_____

_____

(2) A person interested in national information_____

_____

(3) A person interested in cops and robbers _____

_____

(4) A person who likes comedy_____

_____

(5) A person who likes quiz shows_____

_____

From *Reading for Survival in Today's Society,* Volume One. © 1978 Goodyear Publishing Company, Inc.

WEDNESDAY

May 26, 1976

	8 WFAA ABC	4 KDFW CBS	5 KXAS NBC	11 KTVT	13 KERA PBS	39 KXTX
7 00 / 15 / 30 / 45	The A.M. Show / .. / .. / ..	CBS Morning News / .. / ..	Today Show / (7:25) Weather / Today Show	Slam Bang Theater / .. / ..	/ / Newsroom	Tennessee Tuxedo / Mighty Mouse
8 00 / 15 / 30 / 45	Good Morning, America / .. / ..	Captain Kangaroo / .. / ..	(8:25) News / Today Show	Comedy Capers / Dusty's Treehouse	Lilias, Yoga and You / Misterogers' Neighborhood	Lassie and the Ranger / The Lone Ranger
9 00 / 15 / 30 / 45	The Mike Douglas Show / .. / ..	The Price Is Right / .. / ..	Celebrity Sweepstakes / High Rollers	Favorite Martian / Night Gallery	Sesame Street / .. / ..	Father Knows Best / The Lucy Show
10 00 / 15 / 30 / 45	Peppermint Place / Happy Days	Gambit / Love of Life	Wheel of Fortune / Hollywood Squares	The Untouchables / ..	Electric Company / Villa Alegre	Room 222 / The Rock
11 00 / 15 / 30 / 45	Let's Make A Deal / All My Children	Young and The Restless / Search For Tomorrow	Magnificent Marble Machine / Mary Hartman, Mary Hartman	Perry Mason / ..	Sign Off	Charisma / 700 Club
12 00 / 15 / 30 / 45	Ryan's Hope / Rhyme and Reason	Eyewitness News / As the World Turns	Area 5 Texas News / Days of Our Lives	News / Cartoon Carnival		.. / ..
1 00 / 15 / 30 / 45	$20,000 Pyramid / Break The Bank	The Guiding Light	The Doctors	Movie: "The Leather Saint" Paul Douglas John Derek		Mayberry R.F.D. / Bold Ones
2 00 / 15 / 30 / 45	General Hospital / One Life To Live	All In The Family / Match Game '76	Another World	.. / .. / ..		.. / Bugs Bunny
3 00 / 15 / 30 / 45	The Edge of Night / Movie Machine: "Terror In The Sky"	Tattletales / Merv Griffin Show	Somerset / Dinah Shore	Popeye / Banana Splits and Friends		Mickey Mouse Club / Rin Tin Rin
4 00 / 15 / 30 / 45	Leif Erickson Doug McClure Roddy McDowall Keenan Wynn	.. / .. / .. / ..	.. / .. / .. / ..	Flintstones / Gilligan's Island	Misterogers' Neighborhood / Sesame Street	Father Knows Best / Brady Bunch
5 00 / 15 / 30 / 45	News 8: Scene Tonight / Movie: "Trog"	Eyewitness News / Thrillseekers	Weekday / NBC News	Lucy / Dick Van Dyke	.. / Electric Company	Hazel / Hogan's Heroes
6 00 / 15 / 30 / 45	Joan Crawford Michael Gough David Griffin	CBS Evening News / Eyewitness News	Area 5 Texas News / Price Is Right	Bewitched / Adam-12	Zoom / Newsroom	Star Trek / ..
7 00 / 15 / 30 / 45	Bionic Woman / .. / ..	Stranded / .. / ..	Little House On the Prairie / ..	F.B.I. / .. / ..	Masterpiece Theatre: Sunset Song / ..	Andy Griffith / Brady Bunch
8 00 / 15 / 30 / 45	Baretta / .. / ..	Cannon / .. / ..	Sanford and Son / Fay	Family Affair / Beverly Hillbillies	Great Performances: Theater In America "The Patriots" / ..	700 Club / ..
9 00 / 15 / 30 / 45	Starsky and Hutch / .. / ..	The Blue Knight / .. / ..	Hawk / .. / ..	Movie: "Rough Night In Jericho" Dean Martin	.. / .. / ..	.. / The Rock
10 00 / 15 / 30 / 45	News 8: Scene Tonight / Movie: "Cinderfella"	Eyewitness News / The Honeymooners	Area 5 Texas News / Tonight Show	Metroplex News Movie Cont'd. / George Peppard	Behind The Lines / Robert MacNeil Report	Youth On the Move / This Is The Life
11 00 / 15 / 30 / 45	Jerry Lewis Ed Wynn Judith Anderson Anna Marie Alberghetti	CBS Late Movie: "Hallf of Anger" Calvin Lockhart Jeff Bridges	Guest: Ed Bluestone Bud Greenspan	.. / Movie Eleven: "Murder One" Robert Conrad	Sign Off	Big Valley / .. / ..
12 00 / 15 / 30 / 45	.. / News 8: Scene Tonight (Repeat)	Janet MacLachlan / ..	Tomorrow / ..	Howard Duff / ..		Look Up / Sign Off

g. Refer to the **Local Newspaper Scheduled Events** and find in a newspaper each of the sections listed. Use the information given to complete the blanks.

SPORTS
Using the sports section, locate articles about two different kinds of sports. Write the day and time (or approximate time) each was played or will be played.

	DAY	TIME
SPORT 1	_____	_____
SPORT 2	_____	_____

TELEVISION
Using the television guide, write the day and the names and lengths of the programs shown on ABC, CBS, and NBC at 7:00 P.M.

DAY _____

NETWORK_____ PROGRAM _____ LENGTH_____

NETWORK_____ PROGRAM _____ LENGTH_____

NETWORK_____ PROGRAM _____ LENGTH_____

MOVIES
Using the movie advertisements, complete the spaces below with information concerning all G or PG movies listed. Write the time of the first showing.

NAME OF THEATER	STARTING DATE	NAME OF MOVIE	TIME
_____	_____	_____	____
_____	_____	_____	____
_____	_____	_____	____
_____	_____	_____	____

SOCIAL EVENTS
Using the society pages, write the place, day, and time of two scheduled events, such as an open house, a wedding, or a party.

EVENT	PLACE	DAY	TIME
_____	_____	_____	_____
_____	_____	_____	_____
_____	_____	_____	_____

other ideas

A. Have group discussions about the basic purposes of schedules.

B. Make a personal schedule showing time for classes, doing after-school chores, studying, sleeping, watching television, etc. for one week. Add to the schedule at the end of each day. Review the weekly schedule and note heavily active days.

C. Use a bus, train, or airline schedule or a special travel brochure to plan an excursion. Select specific destinations and best routes. Note travel times, need for housing, number of meals while en route, etc.

D. Make a chart of the kinds of schedules used by students in your classroom. Examples are television, movie, football, and transportation schedules.

E. Create a schedule for the ideal day.

F. Prepare a television schedule card. In blank spaces, fill in the names of television programs shown on one channel in your area. Across the top of the card, write times the programs are shown. Call program names from a television newspaper guide, and play the game as you would play Bingo.

G. Prepare a class schedule as a class project.

H. Using a calendar, count how many weekends there are in the school year. How many federal holidays are marked on the calendar?

key words & phrases

arrive	midnight	program	first class
depart	via	freight	passenger
A.M.	priority	direct	tourist class
P.M.	cargo	flight	connection
noon	cancel	fare	services

From *Reading for Survival in Today's Society, Volume One,* ©1978 Goodyear Publishing Company, Inc.

self-evaluation

	date completed	possible score	your score	EXPERT	AVERAGE	FAIR	HELP!
1. Reading airline time schedules		7					
2. Reading symbols on airline schedules		8					
3. Locating information about airline travel		14					
4. Finding information about cost of airline flights		9					
5. Identifying scheduled events in newspapers		14					

CIRCLE **other ideas**
COMPLETED: A B C D E
　　　　　　 F G H

TOTAL
POSSIBLE
POINTS:
52

YOUR
TOTAL
POINTS:

**How did
you rate
yourself?**

name & date

From *Reading for Survival in Today's Society,* Volume One, ©1978 Goodyear Publishing Company, Inc.

magazine facts

4

4

MAGAZINE FACTS

Magazines dealing with every conceivable topic are available at newsstands. The actual number of magazines being published annually is unknown, but *there are over 50 magazines in the United States and Canada with an average circulation exceeding one million.*[1] Obviously, people do read magazines; in fact, *about 60 percent of the adults regularly read one or more weekly or monthly magazines.*[2]

Developing magazine preferences depends on exposure to magazines over a period of time. It is possible that 40 percent of the homes in this country do not have magazines. Unfortunately, most schools have an extremely limited number of magazines available to students, and these are usually found in the library or media center. If students are to become aware of the tremendous amount of information in magazines, magazines must be available in school libraries but also in individual classrooms in sufficient number and kind.

Specific reading lessons emphasized in this module are: (1) locating factual information related to different topics; (2) using advertisements to order; (3) finding facts in advertisements; (4) contrasting facts in magazines; and (5) locating specific facts related to a topic.

materials

Make available in the classroom a number and variety of magazines to be used by students to locate information, to cut out pertinent parts, and to circle and write answers.

---

[1]The Reader's Digest Association, Inc., *Reader's Digest 1975 Almanac and Yearbook* (Pleasantville, N.Y.: The Reader's Digest Association, Inc., 1975), pp. 696–697.

[2]Gordon McCloskey, *Education and Public Understanding* (New York: Harper & Brothers, 1959), p. 102.

survival reading skills

1. LOCATING FACTUAL INFORMATION RELATED TO DIFFERENT TOPICS

Look through magazines until you have located at least one article about each of the topics listed below. Search the article for general factual information about the topic. Complete the outline by writing in the information you find.

I. Health

    A. _____

    B. _____

    C. _____

    D. _____

    E. _____

II. Education

    A. _____

    B. _____

    C. _____

    D. _____

    E. _____

III. A Famous Person

    A. _____

    B. _____

    C. _____

    D. _____

    E. _____

From *Reading for Survival in Today's Society, Volume One,* © Goodyear Publishing Company, Inc.

2. USING ADVERTISTMENTS TO ORDER

Refer to the **Foliage House Plants** order/advertisement and answer the following:

a. How many day's free examination of the book is offered? _____

_____

b. How much does the book cost if you decide to keep it?_____

_____ plus _____

_____

c. If you do not want to keep the book, what must you do? _____

_____

d. When you send for the book, to what else are you agreeing to subscribe?

_____

e. When and how can you cancel your subscription?

When?_____

How?_____

Use this card to get FOLIAGE HOUSE PLANTS

Yes, I would like to examine *Foliage House Plants*. Please send it to me for 10 days' free examination and enter my subscription to the TIME-LIFE ENCYCLOPEDIA OF GARDENING. If I decide to keep *Foliage House Plants*, I will pay $6.95 plus shipping and handling. I then will receive future volumes in the TIME-LIFE ENCYCLOPEDIA OF GARDENING SERIES, shipped a volume at a time approximately every other month. Each is $6.95 plus shipping and handling and comes on a 10-day free examination basis. There is no minimum number of books that I must buy, and I may cancel my subscription at any time simply by notifying you.

If I do not choose to keep *Foliage House Plants*, I will return the book within 10 days, my subscription for future volumes will be canceled, and I will not be under any further obligation.

Name . . . .
(please print)

Address. . . . . .Apt. . . . .

City. . . . . .State . . . . .Zip . . . .

Residents of Canada: Mail form in envelope. **Schools and Libraries:** Order Library Style Bindings from Silver Burdett Co., Morristown, N.J. 07960. Eligible for Titles I, II funds.

WOMAN'S DAY   BQBKW9

3. FINDING FACTS IN ADVERTISEMENTS

Refer to the **Elmer's glue** material and answer the following questions about directions to make the heart shapes:

a. How many pieces of paper should be glued?_____

b. What is the cardboard covered with?_____

c. How many drops of food coloring should be blended?_____

d. What kind of straw do you use?_____

e. What do you mix with the food coloring? _____

f. What kind of glue is recommended? _____

g. What address do you use to order "51 Warm, Wonderful Valentines?"

_____

_____

4. CONTRASTING FACTS IN MAGAZINES

Using magazine articles and/or pictures, locate *facts* only about each of the following topics: a child, a tree, an adult, a flower, a disease, and a health activity. Write or paste the items in the appropriate space below.

A CHILD   AN ADULT

A TREE   A FLOWER

A DISEASE   A HEALTH ACTIVITY

From *Reading for Survival in Today's Society*, Volume One, © 1978 Goodyear Publishing Company, Inc.

5. LOCATING SPECIFIC FACTS RELATED TO A TOPIC

Using magazine articles and/or pictures, locate facts that might be useful to the types of people listed below. Write or paste the facts in the appropriate spaces.

AN ARTIST

A FAMILY WITH 10 CHILDREN

A PERSON WHO WANTS TO LOSE WEIGHT

From *Reading for Survival in Today's Society*, Volume One, ©1978 Goodyear Publishing Company, Inc.

other ideas

A. Compare three or four different magazine covers. Design a cover for a magazine about a topic of interest to you.

B. Find a magazine article that gives a factual description of an object, such as an automobile. Write characteristics given for the object, but do not write the name of the object. Give your list of characteristics to a partner to make a drawing of the object, using only the information given. Compare the finished drawing with the magazine picture or illustration.

C. Find a magazine article that asks a question, such as, "Is Cable Television the Coming Thing?" Underline all the *facts* in the article used to answer the question.

D. Select a magazine article from a news magazine. Read two paragraphs and underline each sentence that contains a fact. Change all of the facts to opinion. Reread the paragraph and notice the change in meaning.

E. Think of some item you would like to sell. Plan and illustrate an advertisement along with an order form.

F. Prepare a set of cards by printing a fact found in a magazine and a number on each. Place them upside down on a game board. The first player picks a fact card, reads it, and tells whether the fact tells who, what, where, when, why, or how. If the answer is correct, the player moves the number of places indicated by the number on the card.

G. Working with a partner, find a fact in a magazine article. Rewrite the fact, leaving out the name of the product. Pass the fact and the closed magazine to another group. Ask the students to read the incomplete fact, look at the table of contents, and see if they can determine which article it came from. (*Variation:* Find a fact in an advertisement. Rewrite it, leaving out the name of the product. Look through the magazine, rather than using the table of contents, to determine which advertisement it came from.)

H. Working with a partner, spend two minutes looking through a magazine to find three facts from three different articles. When you have found your facts, write a short paragraph tying the three facts together. Read your paragraph to the group.

I. Find a fact in a magazine which relates to something you are studying in science or social studies. How does it relate?

From *Reading for Survival in Today's Society*, Volume One, ©1978 Goodyear Publishing Company, Inc.

From *Reading for Survival in Today's Society*, Volume One, ©1978 Goodyear Publishing Company, Inc.

key words & phrases

games	camping	clothing	agriculture
food	music	industry	medicine
teeth	scientific	decorating	government
tools	mechanical	photography	anthropology
pets	history	beverages	electronics

self-evaluation

	date completed	possible score	your score	EXPERT	AVERAGE	FAIR	HELP!
1. Locating factual information related to different topics		**15**					
2. Using advertisements to order		**7**					
3. Finding facts in advertisements		**7**					
4. Contrasting facts in magazines		**6**					
5. Locating specific facts related to a topic		**3**					

CIRCLE other ideas COMPLETED: A B C D E F G H I

TOTAL POSSIBLE POINTS: **38**

YOUR TOTAL POINTS:

How did you rate yourself?

name & date

_____

current events

5

5

CURRENT EVENTS

Apart from conversations, the newspaper still provides the major avenue for communication of the latest developments in almost every area of interest. In 1974, *over 61 million daily newspapers were circulated in the United States*, a fact that gives some indication of the awesome "power of the press."[1] Despite this power, the newspaper remains one of the print bargains in today's society of rising costs and inflated prices. Where else can you purchase the amount of printed information contained in a newspaper for so small a cost?

Approximately 80 percent of the adults in this country take advantage of this bargain by regularly reading one or more daily or weekly newspapers.[2] For many of these people, reading the newspaper means skimming/scanning material until an article or advertisement of particular interest is reached. At that point, more intensive reading skills are used—such skills as locating information, critical analysis, comparison of facts, and prediction, to mention only a few.

Specific reading lessons emphasized in this module are: (1) finding basic information in a lead story; (2) identifying local current events; (3) noting current events in other geographical areas; (4) locating current events about people; and (5) reading about different current events.

materials

> Students should bring copies of newspapers to class. Consider subscribing to a local newspaper, as well as to newspapers from other geographical areas.

[1] United States Bureau of the Census, *Statistical Abstract of the United States: 1975* (96th ed.; Washington, D.C.: U.S. Bureau of the Census, 1975), p. 523.

[2] The Reader's Digest Association, Inc., *Reader's Digest 1975 Almanac and Yearbook* (Pleasantville, N.Y.: The Reader's Digest Association, Inc., 1975), p. 101.

survival reading skills

1. FINDING BASIC INFORMATION IN A LEAD STORY

Locate the front page story that has the largest headline and find answers to each of the following:

a. Where is it located on the page? _____

_____

b. What is the key word or phrase in the headline? _____

_____

c. Who or what is the news story about? _____

_____

d. When did an important event in the story happen? _____

_____

e. Why did that event happen? _____

_____

_____

2. IDENTIFYING LOCAL CURRENT EVENTS

Use a recent newspaper and locate stories about examples of these types of events that happened locally. Write the major theme of the articles.

a. An accident _____

_____

_____

b. A sports event _____

_____

_____

c. A society event _____

_____

_____

d. A pleasant event _____

_____

_____

e. A downtown event _____

_____

_____

3. NOTING CURRENT EVENTS IN OTHER GEOGRAPHICAL AREAS

Use a recent newspaper and locate stories that have a dateline or were written about areas outside your city. Complete the information below:

a. Find an article about another country. The name of the country is

_____,

and the article is about _____

_____.

b. Find an article about another state. The name of the state is _____

_____

and the article is about _____

_____.

c. Find an article about another city. The name of the city is _____

_____,

and the article is about _____

_____.

4. LOCATING CURRENT EVENTS ABOUT PEOPLE

Locate stories in a newspaper about each of the following kinds of people, read the articles, and write the name of the person and his or her accomplishment described in the article.

KIND OF PERSON   PERSON'S NAME   ACCOMPLISHMENT

politician   _____   _____

                   _____   _____

From *Reading for Survival in Today's Society*, Volume One, ©1978 Goodyear Publishing Company, Inc.

sports figure   _____ _____

_____ _____

businessperson   _____ _____

_____ _____

attorney   _____ _____

_____ _____

government official _____ _____

_____ _____

person under 18   _____ _____

_____ _____

5. READING ABOUT DIFFERENT CURRENT EVENTS

Use a recent newspaper and locate stories about some aspect of each of the following topics. Discuss the main points of the articles.

- Health
- Effects of weather
- Changes in regulations or laws
- Law enforcement

other ideas

A. Separate the articles on the front page of a newspaper from their headlines. Place the headlines in an envelope. Trade articles and headlines with a friend and let him try to match each headline with the corresponding article.

B. Organize a school newspaper. Each class should designate a class reporter, and all students should be encouraged to submit articles concerning current events in the school.

C. Invite a reporter from a local newspaper to speak in your class. You might select a story he or she has written, and then discuss how a reporter decides (1) which stories are important and (2) which facts relating to one story are the most important.

D. One of the most difficult tasks of the news reporter is to match the length of his/her article with the printing space available. Select an article in the newspaper which interests you, decide which details mentioned in the article are the *least* important, and shorten the article by 50 words.

From Heading for Survival in Today's Society, Volume One, ©1978 Goodyear Publishing Company, Inc.

E. The three most important parts of a news article are: the headline, the lead (first) sentence, and the first paragraph. If possible, a reporter will try to answer five questions—who, what, when, where, why, and how—in these first parts of a story. Select five marking pens of different colors, one for each question. Use them to underline the answers to each question. For example, you might underline the "who" in yellow, the "what" in red, the "where" in blue, and so on.

F. Generally a newspaper contains four categories of information:

- News stories
- Feature stories, about an unusual or important person or place
- Opinions, such as editorials
- Classified and other ads

Design a bulletin board that illustrates the variety of newspaper information contained in these categories. You may wish to emphasize your theme by covering the board with the "funny papers."

From *Reading for Survival in Today's Society,* Volume One, ©1978 Goodyear Publishing Company, Inc.

key words & phrases

births	television	radio	press release
book reviews	theater	premier	club meeting
obituaries	update	lecture	mail delivery
editorials	price change	recital	political decisions
sports	cartoon	trial	international events

self-evaluation

	date completed	possible score	your score	EXPERT	AVERAGE	FAIR	HELP!
1. Finding basic information in a lead story		5					
2. Identifying local current events		5					
3. Noting current events in other geographical areas		6					
4. Locating current events about people		12					
5. Reading current events about different topics		4					

CIRCLE **other ideas**
COMPLETED: A B C D E
           F

TOTAL POSSIBLE POINTS: **32**

YOUR TOTAL POINTS:

How did you rate yourself?

name & date

newspaper classified information

6

NEWSPAPER CLASSIFIED INFORMATION

For persons wishing to sell items or advertise services, a classified advertisement is probably the least expensive way to reach a large number of people. For persons wishing to purchase goods or services, looking through classified advertisements and catalogs are two of the easiest ways to shop.

Most students are not aware of the content and purpose of classified ads in a newspaper. Many have never looked at even one section of this part of the newspaper. They need to develop a working knowledge of this part of the newspaper to locate bicycles or guitars for sale, apartments for rent, an electrician or plumber, or even a job opening.

Specific reading lessons emphasized in this module are: (1) learning the meaning of selected abbreviations found in classified advertisements; (2) finding basic information in classified advertisements; (3) recognizing specific needs in classified advertisements; (4) locating various services advertised; and (5) categorizing information in classified advertisements.

materials

In addition to this module's examples of different kinds of newspaper classified advertisements, students should collect and bring to class an assortment of classified ads.

survival reading skills

1. LEARNING THE MEANING OF SELECTED ABBREVIATIONS FOUND IN CLASSIFIED ADVERTISEMENTS

Look at various newspaper classified advertisement sections. Below, write twelve different abbreviations found in these advertisements and the meaning of each abbreviation as it is used in classified ads:

ABBREVIATION   MEANING

1._____

2._____

3._____

4._____

5._____

6._____

7._____

8._____

9._____

10._____

11._____

12._____

2. FINDING BASIC INFORMATION IN CLASSIFIED ADVERTISEMENTS

Look in the **Motorcycles** advertisements, locate the answers to the following questions, and write each answer on the appropriate line.

a. What is the most expensive motorcycle for sale?_____

_____

b. Which motorcycle is the least expensive?_____

_____

c. What is the oldest motorcycle for sale? _____

_____

From Reading for Survival in Today's Society, Volume One. © 1978 Goodyear Publishing Company, Inc.

MOTORCYCLES	85

1971 HONDA SL 350, excellent running cond., 489-0682, $350.

1974 550 HONDA, extended front end, high handle bars, 5,000 ml., $1200. 544-1635, 493-1890.

1973 HONDA 350 4 cylinder, runs well, must sell. $725 or best offer. Call 929-5250 Chapel Hill & ask for Steve.

1973 HONDA CL-350, $600. See at JAXON SMALL ENGINE & CYCLE REPAIRS, 1810 Fay St.

'73 SUZUKI PS-125, only 1500 miles, like new, $500. Call 383-4042 after 5.

HARLEY-DAVIDSON: Sportsters, Super Glides, and Electra Glides all at big savings. See us before you buy.
JORDANS INC.
"Franchised dealer for Harley-Davidson and Yamaha Motor Cycles."
625 North Park Ave.,
Burlington, N.C. Phone 227-1261

1975 CB; 750 extended front, Harley rear wheel, Cheeta seat, headers. 682-2101 after 4:30 p.m. & ask for Larry Gibbs. They will page.

1972 SUZUKI TS-125 dirt bike, runs great. $350. Call 383-2652.

1972 SUZUKI, 1,800 miles, $1,000 firm. See at 1951 Cheek Rd. at M F Body Shop.

'73 HONDA CB 350, 7,000 miles, exc. cond. $695, make offer. Tarheel Motor Sales 682-2679, 688-5657.

1973 SUZUKI TS 250. Excellent condition. $580. Call 383-7080 after 6 p.m.

1974 HARLEY DAVIDSON Sportster XL 1000. 3,300 miles. Call 688-1604 after 5 p.m.

1965 HARLEY Davidson Chopper with lots of chrome. Exc. cond. Sharp. 477-8309 or 477-2874 anytime after 5:30.

MOTORCYCLE TRAILER. Excellent shape. $1,500. Ph. 596-7697.

1973 HONDA 450, like new, 4,000 miles. $900. Phone 682-1042.

1974 HONDA CB 360. 5,000 miles. Excellent cond. 2 helmets included. $725. Call 286-7570.

1972 HARLEY DAVIDSON Sportster, elec. star, excellent mechanical cond. 5,000 miles on engine. Must see to appreciate, $2300. After 4 p.m. Mon. thru Fri. — anytime wk-ends. 682-4689.

1970 Honda 350, 383-2480.

'72 TRIUMPH TRIDENT 750, extended front end, pull backs, King-Queen, headers, Harley tires, $1,700 or best offer. 693-5289 after 5:30 Oxford.

d. Which motorcycle has the greatest number of miles on it?_____

_____

e. What telephone number would a person call if he or she wanted more

information about the 1973 Suzuki TS-250 motorcycle? _____

f. Which motorcycle advertisement has the least amount of information

about it? _____

g. What brands does the motorcycle dealer sell?_____

_____

h. After what time should a person call for information about the 1965

Harley Davidson Chopper?_____

3. RECOGNIZING SPECIFIC NEEDS IN CLASSIFIED ADVERTISEMENTS
Refer to the **Unfurnished Apartments** advertisements and answer the following questions:

a. If you wanted an apartment for the summer only, which telephone num-

ber would you call? _____

From *Reading for Survival in Today's Society*, Volume One, ©1978 Goodyear Publishing Company, Inc.

UNFURNISHED APTS. 19

2 BR MODERN, refrigerator & stove, all conveniences, private entrances, fenced dog run. 688-3136.

SUMMER STUDENTS! We are now subletting apts. for summer ranging from $135. to $180 mo., and also taking applications to reserve apts. for fall. Call today! HUDSON REALTY 477-1070.

COLONY MANOR

Wake Forest Hwy. Convenient to Wellons Village Shopping Center & NCCU, 2 bedroom units, air conditioned, stove, refrigerator, (Genneral Electric), shag carpet, laundry room, pool & club house maintenance. Lease Furniture by Metrolease. Call Resident Manager — 596-9463.

3 BR TOWNHOUSE, new carpet, 1½ baths, central heat & AC. Also 2 BR apt., 1½ baths. 596-6582.

● **APARTMENTS** ●
● **489-9688** ●

CROASDAILE & CARVER Apts. 1, 2 & 3 bdrm. garden & townhouse units. Garden View Realty, 383-5575.

CARRIAGE HOUSE APARTMENTS

1, 2, 3-bedroom units
a prestige Durham address
$175 to $245
North on Roxboro Rd. (U. S. 501)
Open: Mon.-Fri. 10-5—Sat. & Sun. 2-4
Res. Mgr. 477-6501

APARTMENTS
1-2-3 Bedrooms

Features include applainces, drapes, carpet, air cond. Good location all over town. Call:

APARTMENT SHOP
1809 CHAPEL HILL RD.
489-6578

1 BEDROOM, quiet location, near Duke, pool, phone 383-5384.

LARGE ROOM for rent. Bath & shower, walk-in closet, off-street parking. Near Wellons Village. 688-6422, 688-4770.

UNFURNISHED ALL electric 1 & 2 bedroom apts. for rent. Under market value. 286-3172.

SPARKLING 1-BR apts. $130 per mo. Very spacious with large walk-in closets. Call 682-0524.

HOLLY HILL APTS.
Luxury
2 Bedroom Units
Carpet — Drapes
Patio — Pool
Near Duke
383-1351

VILLA APARTMENTS
1505 Duke University Road
Excellent Location

These one-bedroom apts. have a most attractive exterior and modern interior. Interior includes stove, refrigerator, disposal, carpet, drapes, air condition, seprate dining area and bath. Swmming pool and laundry facilities are located on premises. Water is included. Located onlp minutes from Duke University, VA & Watts Hospital.

Call today for Appointment.

Roberts Associates   683-1541

APT. LOCATOR SERVICE
Take advantage of the most comprehensive unaffiliated apt. location service in the Durham-Chapel Hill area. Choose your apt. through characteristic selection, using our punched card system . . . A FREE service of Metrolease. Ph. 493-1491 for details.

b. If you wanted a one-bedroom apartment with a swimming pool near Watts Hospital, which apartments would you call?_____

c. If you wanted to look at the advertised apartment for which the most features are listed, what telephone number would you call? _____

_____

d. What features are listed for the large room for rent near Wellons Village?

_____

_____

e. What telephone number would you call to get someone to help you locate an apartment?_____

Is there a charge for this service? _____

From *Reading for Survival in Today's Society*, Volume One, ©1978 Goodyear Publishing Company, Inc.

SERVICES OFFERED 45

CARPENTRY
CARPENTRY, ROOFING, painting, guttering. Free estimates. Ph. 477-2025.

CARPET CLEANING
Rent A Steam Carpet Shampooer McBroom's Rentals 2334 Guess Rd.

CAMERA REPAIRS
CUSTOM WORK. Obsolete and antique cameras a specialty. Call Leon's anytime Sun. thru Thurs. 477-5354.

CHILD CARE
TEACHER WITH 2 daughters would like to keep girls ages 4 to 11 in her home this summer. Call Poplar Apts. 383-5960.

FIRST CHRISTIAN Church is now accepting applications for enrollment for child care — infants thru kindergarten. 682-6498 days, even. 477-8662.

WILL KEEP infants & small children in my home, Lakewood area Ph. 489-8269.

I WILL keep children in my home E. Club & Bragtown area. 477-0873.

REGISTERED DAY care center, 21 yrs. experience. Infants on up. Bragtown area. 477-2923.

Will keep children in my home. Ph. 544-7170.

REGISTER NOW for our summer & fall program — ages 2½ to 6. We also have a summer program for school age children. Come by or phone Grace Baptist Day Care Center, 682-0671. Open from 6:30 a.m. to 6 p.m.

CLEANING
CLEAN GUTTERS, thin out wooded areas & haul away. Also tree & lawn work & spraying. 596-4665 day or night.

SERVICES OFFERED 45

WILL WASH aluminum siding with contract. Call Bill Menter for professional service, 471-2069.

GORMAN BAPTIST Kinder Kare Center Kindergarten & care for age 3-5. Loc. on E. Geer St. (I-85 & Red Mill Rd.) 688-3947.

CONCRETE WORK
CONCRETE WORK professionally done. Lge. slabs, porches, sidewalks, driveways & patch work, etc. Watkins Concrete Contractor 477-8914 or 477-1828.

CONCRETE WORK — Reasonable rates. Driveways, walkways, patios & back hoe service. Ph. Piedmont Concrete Co. for free estimate 682-5193.

DRIVEWAY, WALKWAY, patio & back hoe service. Raymond Hales, 286-4417.

DOZER & LOADER WORK
ALL KINDS land clearing, stump removal, trash hauling. Rich top soil. 688-2252.

DRAIN WORK
DRAIN WORK for under-house wetness, lawn drainage, downspout drain work, etc. Call 596-4665 anytime

ELECTRICAL REPAIRS
ELECTRICIAN — 20 yrs. experience working from home. Specializing in small jobs. Available evenings & weekends. Save some money. 688-6973 8 a.m.-11 p.m.

FLOOR COVERING
CUSTOM FLOORING, all types of flooring installation, quality work, guaranteed to customer satisfaction, 599-9527 or 599-0336 Roxboro for free estimates.

SERVICES OFFERED 45

FURNACE SERVICE
SAVE FUEL! Have your furnace serviced and vacuumed now. Call DAUGHTRY HEATING CO., 477-4089.

HAULING
WILL HAUL any junk or trash. $10-$15 per pickup load. Also will move furniture $15-$25. Call anytime 682-9082.

MOWING LAWNS, hauling, cleaning out basements & tearing down old bldgs. Call 596-5462.

HOME IMPROVEMENTS
REMODELING AND building of all types, seamless gutters, roofing. Quality work at a price you can afford. Call 493-1534 for a free estimate.

JUNK CAR HAULING
WILL MOVE OLD CARS FREE. With or without tires. Phone 682-4945.

LANDSCAPING
STUMPS REMOVED below ground with modern equipment. Reasonable rates. General Spray & Landscape Service, 477-8676

TREE REMOVAL, TRACTOR WORK, HAULING, PINE BARK MULCH FOR SALE. Call 596-5166.

LANDSCAPING TREE work, shrubbery trimmings, drain pipes, trash hauling, gutter & yard cleaning, etc. W E. Ferrell, 682-9067

LAWN CARE
LAWN WORK of all types. Stump removal, top soil, backhoe & grading work. 688-2252, 682-4945.

SERVICES OFFERED 45

LAWN CARE: Cutting grass, yards, etc., any size — no job too large or small. Ph. 544-2873, Donald Fields.

THRIFTY LAWN CUTTING SERVICE 688-8920

LAWN MOWER REPAIR
REPAIR AT your home or free pickup. Roto-Tillers & riding tractors. 477-6176 btw. 7 a.m.-til 10.

MANSONRY
Masonry work. 25 yrs. experience. Call 682-0938.

MOVING
DO IT yourself & save money. Truck & Trailers Renting. MCBROOM'S RENTALS. 2334 Guess Road. 286-4414.

PAINTING
J. W. Maynard & Son "For Professional Results" Ph. 471-3333 REPAIRS—REMODELING—ADDITION A. N. CARPENTER 477-7031 AFTER 6 P.M.

SOBER PAINTERS, family men also complete decorating services, free estimates, of course. Haslam Interiors & Exteriors. We appreciate your business. 383-5356 or 688-0390.

PAINTING & PAPERING of all kinds. Also small repairs. Free estimates. All jobs priced reasonably. 477-1282 anytime.

SUMMER PAINTING, carpentry, masonry, concrete, roofing & plastering. Call Bill Shepard 596-4089, Free estim.

BUTNER PAINT Company. Interior Exterior Work done, fully insured. 575-6079.

4. LOCATING VARIOUS SERVICES ADVERTISED

Refer to the **Services Offered** classified advertisements and answer the following:

a. Dirt spilled on your den carpet when a plant container broke. You do not want to replace the carpet. What is the name of a business you might call?_____

b. A friend needs a child care center for his nine-month-old child. What telephone numbers might he call? _____

c. A neighbor wants to have some trees removed that have pine beetle disease. He also wants to buy some pine bark mulch. What telephone number could he call?_____

From *Reading for Survival in Today's Society*, Volume One, ©1978 Goodyear Publishing Company, Inc.

d. The lawn mower is broken. What telephone number might you call?

_____

e. You want to have three electrical outlets added in your home. What

telephone number might you call? _____

5. CATEGORIZING INFORMATION IN CLASSIFIED ADVERTISEMENTS

a. Working in groups, use the **Automobiles for Sale** and **Sports & Foreign Cars** classified advertisements on page 62 to complete the outline given below by listing the names of three automobiles that belong in each category. Using *only* the information given in the advertisement, decide which of the three cars in each category seems to be the best buy. Circle the name of that car. Be prepared to give reasons for your selections.

I. Compact Automobiles for Sale

A. _____

B. _____

C. _____

II. Middle-sized Automobiles for Sale

A. _____

B. _____

C. _____

AUTOMOBILES FOR SALE 89

71 FIREBIRD Pontiac, A-T, A-C, tape, 29,570 miles. Runs good, $1475. 471-3333.

WANTED: SAAB 96, 1969-1972, must be in good working order & appearance, $1350 maximum, 833-6360 Ral.

1970 PLY. SATELLITE. 4 Dr., A.T., P.S., A-C, W.S.W. radial tires. 286-1327 after 6 p.m.

'69 BARRACUDA 383 Magnum, 3 spd. trans., Crager wheels, $1,200 528-2205 after 6:30 p.m.

1973 GRAN TORINO, AC, AT, PS, PB, R & H, vinyl top, extras, $2,200 477-0055.

74 Eldorado, loaded, white, half top, red inter., 23,000 miles, tape player, $6995.

COLCLOUGH AUTO SALES
612 Rigsbee Ave.   Dr. 5109   682-9275

**WE BUY
USED CARS**
CARPENTER'S CHEVROLET
Durham, N.C.
682-0451

1965 LINCOLN Continental Luxury sedan, full power, good cond., $395. 489-5105.

1974 VOLKSWAGON bus, 25,000 miles, like new, 1 owner, AM-FM, blue with white top. Call Frank Seamster, Triangle Volkswagon, 489-2371.

HICK'S USED CARS
820 Morgan St.   Dlr. 4379

WE BUY and sell Imported and domestic automobiles
TRIANGLE VW-PORSCHE-AUDI
489-2371   Dlr. 1345

'70 TOYOTA Corona, 4 dr. sedan, auto trans., 48,000 mi. original owner, good tires. 688-6278.

CITY MOTORS
1305 Avondale Dr. No. 25   Ph. 688-7126
74 Ranger XLT. Loaded $3695
74 Ranger. Loaded $3595
72 Sport Cust. AT, PS, PB $2195
72 Chev. C-10, AT, PS, PB $1895
68 Torino GT, HT, FP, Air $995
72 Torino GS, 4 spd $1695
(2) 5 H.P. Clark Tillers ..... At Cost
71 Travco 22' motor home
73 Executive 26' motor home

'72 SS CHEVELLE, AC, PS, PB, AT, AM, 8-tract stereo, 350 V-8, $2300 or best offer. 477-4355.

1973 CADILLAC Coupe DeVille, low mileage, like new steel radials, $4,000. Will negotiate. 489-7962 after 6 p.m.

'72 LINCOLN Continental. Immaculate throughout, white on white, red int., loaded. Nicest Lincoln in town. $3295. Tarheel Motor Sales 682-2679, 688-5657.

73 BUICK Limited. 40-60 seats, AM-FM stereo, tape player, cruise control, full power. Good cond. Call 682-8000 or inquire 821 N. Miami Blvd.

CITY MOTORS
1305 Avondale Dr.   No. 25   Ph. 688-7126

70 Torino Brougham 4 dr. HT, FP . $695
71 Dart Swinger HT, V8, AT $1095
72 Pinto, AT, yellow fin $995
69 Cut. Conv. AT, FP $495
67 Comet 2 dr., 6 cyl $395
70 Malibu SS, AT, FP $1095
65 Nova 4 dr., 6 cyl $345

65 BUICK Skylark, new paint, PS, AT, bucket seats. See at 2409 E. Main St Apt. B.

1968 FURY III, good condition, $400. Ph. 596-1648 or 682-0146.

'73 ROAD RUNNER, 45,000 miles, 318 cu. in. motor. 489-9633 after 4:30.

1976 MUSTANG Cobra II, V-6, 4 spd., radial tires, $4,900 or best offer. 596-5903.

1959 FORD Retractable, 818 Cleveland St. Daytime only.

1968 PONTIAC CATALINA 4 dr. h.t., A.T., p.s., p.b., A-C, radial tires, good cond. See & make offer. 471-1205.

$2,500. 1972 Chevrolet Monte Carlo. Automatic, power steering, power brakes, air conditioned, tape stereo, clean, good tires & good condition 2210 Sparger Rd. Ph. 383-2757.

1971 FURY. $900. $400 down. Ph. 682-0146.

III. Large Automobiles for Sale

A. _____

B. _____

C. _____

SPORTS & FOREIGN CARS 91

74 FIAT 124 Sedan, AT, 12,000 miles. Exc. cond. 30 mpg. Driven only 6 mos. Must be seen. $2,700. 286-9421.

VW VAN, 1973, 9 passenger, exc. cond. New paint, radial tires, $2450. Call nights 929-2870, Chapel Hill.

1970 AUDI 100 LS, 4 dr. sedan, good cond., $1500, Hillsborough, 732-7605.

MUST SELL
240 Z 1973, air, AM-FM stereo, chrome wheels, will accept first reasonable offer. Dealers welcome. Ph. 682-6505.

1970 MGB red convertible, 4 speed & radio. Call 477-0260.

'72 CORVETTE convertible. Immaculate. Ph. days 929-5911 or evenings 929-2288 Chapel Hill.

1959 CORVETTE, good condition. Must sell, $2,700. Ph. 596-7765.

1970 VW super beetle, low mileage, good AM-FM, Michelin radials, ex. cond., $1,500, 477-1764.

1969 TOYOTA CORONA. 4 Dr., A.T., must be seen & driven to be appreciated. Call 477-5500 wk. ends & after 5 wk. days.

'69 VW Squareback. Good condition. New paint. $895. Ph. 682-8896.

'74 VW Super Beetle, light blue, 24,000 miles, new radials, extra clean. 383-7060.

1971 AUDI 100 LS. Low mileage, new paint. Exc. cond. Serious Inquiries only. Ph. 493-2589.

'66 CORVETTE parts. 427-425 motor, 4 sp. transmission, 411 positive tract., seats, big block, hood, all interior parts. Call after 5, 471-3557.

BUG! 1970 VW, great condition. New battery. Newly tuned. Half year warranty. 684-6383.

1975 FIAT X19, ex. cond., low mileage, bet. 9-5, 682-9229, after 6 & wknds., 471-2882.

'73 CORVETTE conv., AT, PS, AM-FM, tape player, good cond., $5,600, 489-2110.

'72 FIAT 850 Sport convertible, 40 mpg, $2,500 or best offer. Call 929-8112.

'69 VW Squareback w-AM-FM, new tires in good cond. but needs some eng. work. $400 below NADA. Call 383-1694.

1970 AUDI Super 90 4-speed, 2 door, AM-FM, 47,000 miles, $895. 471-2060 & 688-4024.

1973 SUPER Beetle 4-speed, radio, $1450. 471-2060 & 688-4024.

1972 MGB, exc. cond. Radio, reduced for quick sale. $2400. Phone 489-4338.

1970 Toyota. $900. Ph. 682-0146.

1971 MERCEDES 300 SEL, beige w-red interior, 57,000 miles, immaculate, factory fitted options, include air suspension, electric sun roof, PW, self scanning grand prix radio, alloy wheels, leather upholstery. $7,500. Call 544-3952, evenings & wk. ends.

1972 VW super beetle Low mileage, good condition, $1,650. 493-3511 ext. 327 or 489-6912.

'71 VW Karman Ghia. Blue, tires almost new, AC, AM-FM, tach. Best offer 596-1391 days, Hillsb. 732-7212 nights, Dennis Denton.

'75 CORVETTE conv. 350, 4 spd, trans., AC, AM-FM stereo w-8 track, American mags w-new Goodyear radials, 286-2319 after 6:30, if no answer call 596-4033 leave message.

1974 PORSCHE 914 2.0 Litre, silver metallic paint, AM-FM radio, 489-0632 anytime.

'74 VOLVO 144 GL, 4 spd. — OD, AC, AM-FM stereo, sunroof, metallic gold, immaculate, 286-3789.

1965 VW VAN, dent & body rust runs well, needs some work. Asking $300, negotiable. Call 688-2760 after 5.

'74 TOYOTA Corona, 4 spd., AC, immaculate cond. $2,900. Mr. Williams 489-8746 or 688-1331.

b. Locate three advertisements that have several abbreviations and paste them in the space below. Rewrite the advertisements using words for each abbreviation.

other ideas

A. Write a classified advertisement offering a service you could perform.

B. Discuss whether anyone in the class has ever used the classified ads and for what purpose.

C. If your class or school writes a newspaper, add a classified section to it. If you do not write a newspaper, develop a classified advertisement pamphlet to be distributed.

D. Pretend that you have a job earning $600 a month. You are not married. Using the classified ads, circle all apartments you could, or would, possibly consider renting. Which would be your first choice? Why? What percentage of your salary would the rental fee be?

E. Turn to the advertisements for **Houses for Sale**. Select several houses that are advertised. Draw a line through all the statements that are opinions. Read what remains.

F. Select any classified ad and rewrite it using as many antonyms as possible. How does the meaning change?

G. Select a classified advertisement category in which several alternatives are presented. If you were going to inquire about one of these ads, which one would you select? Why? What do you feel should be included to make an ad appealing?

key words & phrases

skilled	license	experience	position
ambition	inquire	immediately	administrator
require	opportunity	supervisor	management
repair	franchise	training	advancement
benefits	executive	graduate	employer

self-evaluation

	date completed	possible score	your score	EXPERT	AVERAGE	FAIR	HELP!
1. Learning the meaning of selected abbreviations found in classified advertisements		12					
2. Finding basic information in classified advertisements		8					
3. Recognizing specific needs in classified advertisements		6					
4. Locating various services advertised		5					
5. Categorizing information in classified advertisements		12					

CIRCLE **other ideas**
COMPLETED: A B C D E
F G

TOTAL POSSIBLE POINTS: **43**

YOUR TOTAL POINTS:

How did you rate yourself?

name & date

From *Reading for Survival in Today's Society,* Volume One. ©1978 Goodyear Publishing Company, Inc.

weather reports

7

WEATHER REPORTS

Weather affects all aspects of our daily lives from the clothing we wear to the kind of recreation we can enjoy. Rain can dampen a parade, call a baseball game, cancel a picnic, or turn would-be golfers into bowlers. And being caught in a downpour, completely unprepared, can be an unpleasant experience indeed! Although not always accurate, weather forecasts do enable persons who read or hear them, and *understand* them, to adjust their daily activities to take advantage of fair weather and lessen the impact of inclement weather. Weather bureau warnings to those in the probable paths of tornadoes and hurricanes have made life-saving precautions possible.

Specific reading skills emphasized in this module are: (1) reading brief weather paragraph summaries; (2) contrasting weather predictions for different localities within a state; (3) locating weather information concerning different places in the country; (4) interpreting symbols in weather reports; and (5) comparing national and international weather predictions.

materials

Suggest students collect and bring to class examples of local, state, national, and international weather forecasts. Organize displays illustrating the various ways weather and its effects are described and depicted in photographs, articles, and graphs.

survival reading skills

1. READING BRIEF WEATHER PARAGRAPH SUMMARIES
Read the weather forecast **"Sunny"** and answer the following:

   a. What is the chance of rain?_____

   b. What are the predicted extremes of temperature?_____

   c. What was the temperature Thursday at 6:00 P.M.?_____

   d. If you wanted more information concerning the weather forecast, on what

   page would you look? _____

**2. CONTRASTING WEATHER PREDICTIONS FOR DIFFERENT
LOCALITIES WITHIN A STATE**
Read the **"California Forecasts"** weather report and answer the following
questions:
   a. What is the predicted high temperature in

   (1) Los Angeles? _____

   (2) The mountains? _____

   (3) The beaches?_____

   (4) The deserts?_____

   (5) San Gabriel Valley?_____

   b. How much warmer may the temperature be on Friday in the deserts?

   _____

   c. What is the smog forecast for the Los Angeles area? _____

   _____

   d. In the marine forecast, winds are predicted at _____

   _____ knots tonight.

Sunny

Sunny today, fair and cool tonight with 10 per cent chance of rain. High, 58, low, 36. (Map and details, Page 2A.)

Thursday Temperatures

8 a.m. 55	12 noon 65	4 p.m. 70
10 a.m. 61	2 p.m. 69	6 p.m. 66

California Forecasts

SOUTHLAND FORECAST

LOS ANGELES: Cloudy today with a chance of occasional light rain. Partly cloudy tonight and Friday morning, becoming sunny Friday afternoon. Highs both days in the mid 60s.

BEACHES: Cloudy with a chance of occasional light rain today. Highs today 58 to 64. Water, 57.

MOUNTAINS: Mostly cloudy with light rain today. Partly cloudy tonight and Friday morning with a chance of a few showers mainly over the southern mountains. Mostly sunny Friday afternoon. Highs today 45 to 52 and Friday 50 to 58. Lows tonight 34 to 40.

SAN FERNANDO VALLEY: Mostly cloudy with a chance of occasional light rain today. Partly cloudy tonight and Friday morning with a chance of light rain near the mountains. Sunny Friday afternoon. Highs both days in the mid to upper 60s.

SAN GABRIEL VALLEY: Mostly cloudy with a chance of occasional light rain today. Partly cloudy tonight and Friday morning with a chance of light rain near the mountains. Sunny Friday afternoon. Highs both days in the mid to upper 60s.

SAN BERNARDINO-RIVERSIDE: Mostly cloudy with a chance of occasional light rain today. Partly cloudy tonight and Friday morning with a chance of light rain near the mountains. Sunny Friday afternoon. Highs both days in the mid to upper 60s.

ORANGE COUNTY: Cloudy with a chance of occasional light rain today. Highs today 58 to 64.

UPPER AND LOWER DESERTS: Variable high cloudiness today and tonight with a slight chance of a few showers over the northern deserts this afternoon. Fair and warmer Friday. Highs today 62 to 72 in the upper deserts and 74 to 80 in the lower deserts. About 2 degrees warmer Friday.

SAN DIEGO COUNTY: Increasing cloudiness today with a chance of light rain Friday morning, clearing and becoming sunny Friday afternoon.

EXTENDED FORECAST

SOUTHERN CALIFORNIA COASTAL AND MOUNTAIN AREAS: Extended outlook Saturday through Monday. Fair and mild Saturday through Monday. High temperatures 65 to 75 coastal areas and in the 50s mountains. Overnight lows 45 to 55 coastal areas and 25 to 35 mountains.

MARINE FORECAST

POINT CONCEPTION TO MEXICAN BORDER AND 60 MILES OUT: Mostly south to southwest winds 5 to 15 knots increasing to 10 to 20 knots this morning. Winds turning westerly 10 to 20 knots this afternoon and west to northwest 8 to 18 knots tonight. Two- to 4-foot wind waves today. Increasing westerly swells to be 5 to 7 feet today with high surf. Showers spreading over area and partly cloudy tonight.

WESTERN FORECASTS

SAN FRANCISCO BAY AREA: Showers again today with a chance of showers tonight becoming partly cloudy Friday. Highs today and Friday in the mid to upper 50s.

SIERRA NEVADA: Showers of rain or snow with chance of thunderstorms today and tonight. Partly cloudy Friday. Strong gusty southerly winds decreasing tonight. Colder.

SAN JOAQUIN VALLEY: Showers likely today and tonight. Partly cloudy Friday. Highs today and Friday in the upper 50s to mid 60s.

SANTA MARIA-SAN LUIS OBISPO COASTAL AREA: Showers today and a chance of showers tonight becoming partly cloudy Friday. Highs today and Friday in the upper 50s to mid 60s.

MONTEREY BAY AREA: Showers likely today and partly cloudy tonight and Friday with chance of showers tonight. Highs today and Friday in the mid 50s to low 60s.

Smog Forecast

There are no health advisories predicted today for the Los Angeles basin. There will be little or no smog in the basin and visibility will be approximately 7 miles.

The Weather

It'll Be A Mite Cooler

The Charlotte Area

Sunny and cool today and Saturday with the highs both days in the upper 50s. Fair and cool tonight with lows in the upper 30s. Chance of rain 10 per cent through tonight. Northerly winds 10 to 20 m.p.h. today.

The Carolinas

BEACHES: Sunny and cool today and Saturday. Fair tonight. Highs today will be in the middle 50s to mid-60s. Lows tonight will be in the middle 30s to low 40s. Chance of rain is 10 per cent today and tonight. Winds are north at 10 to 20 m.p.h. today.

MOUNTAINS: Sunny and cool today and Saturday with the highs in the middle 50s to about 60. Lows tonight will be in the upper 20s to middle 30s. Chance of rain is 10 per cent today and tonight.

SOUTH CAROLINA: Mostly sunny and cooler today with the high in the upper 60s. Fair and cold tonight with the low in the upper 30s inland to the low 40s along the coast. Fair and mild Saturday with highs in the 60s. Chance of rain is near zero today and tonight. Northerly winds 15 to 20 m.p.h. today, diminishing tonight.

EXTENDED FORECAST

NORTH CAROLINA: Fair Saturday and Sunday, becoming partly cloudy Monday with a chance of showers in the west portion of the state. Unseasonably cool Saturday with highs in the mid-50s to low 60s. Lows in the 20s in the mountains to the upper 30s along the coast. Temperatures moderating Sunday and Monday. High both days is expected to be in the mid-to-upper 60s. Low in the low to mid-40s.

SOUTH CAROLINA: Generally fair with cool nights and mild days. Low in the 30s early Saturday rising to around 50 by Monday. High mostly in the 60s Saturday, climbing to the 70s by Monday.

NATIONAL EXTREMES

The warmest spot in the nation was Homestead, Fla., at 83 degrees, and the coolest spot was Bradford, Pa., at 31 degrees.

Drawing by Jimmy Jackson, 9, of Hickory Grove Elementary School, Charlotte.

YESTERDAY AND TODAY IN THE NATION

Light rain stretched along the Pacific Coast from Washington to Southern California Thursday. A trough of low pressure in the eastern Pacific and a cold front combined to trigger the precipitation. There were two other main areas of precipitation in the country. The first included drizzle and rain that extended from the central high Plains to central Nebraska and northeast Kansas. The other area consisted of rain showers in Northern Florida. There were some spotty areas of rain over Eastern North Carolina, southeast Pennsylvania, southwest Oklahoma and north-central Texas. Rain is forecast today for parts of Washington, Oregon and California. Much of the remainder of the country should have fair weather.

FORECAST for Friday

Snow, Flurries, Rain, Showers

Cold, Warm, Stationary, Occluded

Figures show high temperatures for area

Data from NATIONAL WEATHER SERVICE NOAA US Dept of Commerce

CAROLINAS WEATHER

	Sky Cover	Temp at 2 pm	24h r. low ending at 8 am
Charlotte	sc cld	69	41
Asheville	sc cld	67	31
Fayetteville	ptcldy	71	49
Greensboro	sc cld	68	35
Hickory	clear	73	39
Raleigh	ptcldy	71	40
Columbia	cldy	74	59
Charleston	cldy	72	47
Greer	sc cld	71	50

TRAVELERS' WEATHER

	Thursday Temperatures H L	Weather	Today's H L
Atlanta	72 42	sunny	65 40
Boise	71 41	ptcldy	61 38
Boston	80 58	fair	83 60
Chicago	45 36	sunny	49 43
Cleveland	46 29	ptcldy	51 35
Ft. Worth	70 45	fair	73 48
Denver	59 38	sunny	65 39
Detroit	53 30	ptcldy	59 36
Helena	70 40	cldy	60 35
Jacksonvl.	72 52	cldy	71 44
Las Vegas	78 50	fair	75 49
Ltle. Rock	71 39	ptcldy	69 43
Los Ang.	67 47	fair	67 48
Louisvle.	65 35	sunny	61 42
Miami	83 65	ptcldy	79 63
Milwaukee	50 31	sunny	63 37
Nashville	68 34	fair	64 39
N. Orleans	79 50	fair	75 49
New York	55 36	sunny	48 38
Orlando	74 58	cldy	74 52
Phila.	57 35	sunny	54 35
Phoenix	85 56	fair	84 55
Ptsbgh.	49 28	sunny	48 35
Richmond	66 36	sunny	57 31
S. F'cisco	58 48	ptcldy	62 48
Seattle	56 42	shwrs	55 42
St. Louis	61 36	sunny	69 47
Tampa	76 59	cldy	75 52
Wash.,D.C	61 38	sunny	56 35

CLIMATE DATA

CHARLOTTE TEMPERATURES: Thursday: High, 71, Low, 45, Mean, 54, Normal, 59. Record high for the day 89. Record low for the day, 25.
SUN SETS today at 6:51 p.m. and rises Saturday at 5:59 a.m.
MOON RISES today at 1:44 p.m. and sets at 2:22 a.m.
PRECIPITATION Thursday in Charlotte 0. Total this month .04; total this year, 7.42; departure from normal this month, .98; excess from normal this year, 5.46.
HUMIDITY at 1 p.m. 37; at 7 p.m. 23.

TODAY'S TIDES

Charleston
High 2:40 a.m.   High 3:21 p.m.
Low 9:13 a.m.   Low 9:39 p.m.
Myrtle Beach
High 2:13 a.m.   High 2:54 p.m.
Low 8:46 a.m.   Low 9:12 p.m.
Carolina Beach
High 1:52 a.m.   High 2:33 p.m.
Low 8:35 a.m.   Low 9:01 p.m.

3. LOCATING WEATHER INFORMATION CONCERNING DIFFERENT PLACES IN THE COUNTRY

Read the weather forecast **"It'll Be a Mite Cooler"** and answer the following:

a. What are the predicted low temperatures in the mountains? _____

At the beaches? _____

b. What is the difference between the high and low temperature predicted for "today" in each of the following cities:

(1) Atlanta? _____

(2) Las Vegas? _____

(3) Richmond? _____

(4) Phoenix? _____

(5) St. Louis? _____

(6) Washington, D.C.? _____

(7) Denver? _____

(8) Ft. Worth? _____

c. What was the humidity at 1:00 P.M. in Charlotte? _____

d. Where was the warmest spot in the nation? _____

e. Where was the coolest spot in the nation? _____

4. INTERPRETING SYMBOLS IN WEATHER REPORTS

The illustration entitled **"Weather Reports, Forecasts"** includes a small chart that defines ten of the most commonly used weather symbols. Use this chart to complete the items below. (If you are not familiar with the names of the states, you may also need an atlas.)

a. Name the northernmost city in California that received rain. _____

_____

b. Name two other states that received rain.

(1) _____

(2) _____

c. Name the city in Texas that had cloudy skies. _____

From Reading for Survival in Today's Society, Volume One, ©1978 Goodyear Publishing Company, Inc.

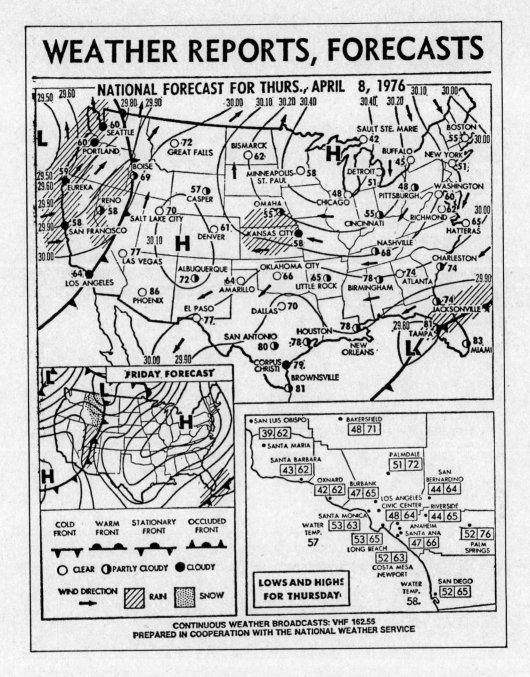

WEATHER REPORTS, FORECASTS

NATIONAL FORECAST FOR THURS., APRIL 8, 1976

FRIDAY FORECAST

| COLD FRONT | WARM FRONT | STATIONARY FRONT | OCCLUDED FRONT |

○ CLEAR   ◑ PARTLY CLOUDY   ● CLOUDY

WIND DIRECTION ➡   ▨ RAIN   ▦ SNOW

LOWS AND HIGHS FOR THURSDAY:

CONTINUOUS WEATHER BROADCASTS: VHF 162.55
PREPARED IN COOPERATION WITH THE NATIONAL WEATHER SERVICE

d. Name three cities along the eastern seaboard that had partly cloudy skies.

(1) _____

(2) _____

(3) _____

From *Reading for Survival in Today's Society*, Volume One, ©1978 Goodyear Publishing Company, Inc.

e. The only type of *front* illustrated on this map is the _____ front.

f. Which direction was the wind blowing in Kansas?_____

g. The large *H* on the map indicates a high pressure zone. What do you think the large *L* indicates?_____

h. How would you describe the sky over Boston?_____

5. **COMPARING NATIONAL AND INTERNATIONAL WEATHER PREDICTIONS**
Read the **"Wednesday's Temperatures"** chart and answer the following questions:

a. In the "Local Temperatures" section, where were the highest maximum temperatures recorded? _____

b. Which city was cooler, Long Beach or Torrance?_____

c. In the "Temperatures and Precipitation over the Far West" section, how many places had rain? _____

d. In the "Temperatures and Precipitation over the Nation" section, what was the difference between the maximum and minimum temperatures of:

    (1) Anchorage? _____

    (2) Albany?_____

    (3) Columbus, Ohio?_____

    (4) El Paso?_____

    (5) Miami Beach?_____

    (6) Syracuse?_____

e. In the same section, which city was warmer, San Antonio or Houston?

_____

    Which city was cooler, Des Moines or Oklahoma City?_____

f. In the "Foreign Cities" section, what was the coolest city?_____

_____

    The warmest city?_____

From *Reading for Survival in Today's Society, Volume One*, ©1978 Goodyear Publishing Company, Inc.

Wednesday's Temperatures

LOCAL TEMPERATURES

Maximum and minimum temperatures at Southern California points, as reported to the Los Angeles office of the National Weather Service, were as follows:

Station—	Max.	Min.
Los Angeles	68	47
Los Angeles Airport	67	50
Bakersfield	75	52
Barstow-Daggett	80	49
Beverly Hills	66	42
Big Bear Lake	60	24
Bishop	70	31
Blythe	82	49
Catalina Avalon	76	46
Culver City	68	49
El Centro	80	48
Fresno	73	44
Hollywood-Burbank	71	46
Lake Arrowhead	58	32
Lake Elsinore	78	40
Lancaster	72	47
Long Beach	71	34
Needles	82	50
Newport Beach	64	48
Northridge	73	42
Ontario	75	42
Palm Springs	82	52
Pasadena	73	44
Riverside U C	74	43
San Bernardino	71	40
San Diego	67	51
San Gabriel	73	48
Santa Ana	72	41
Santa Barbara	66	43
Santa Maria	69	47
Santa Monica	65	48
Simi Hills	64	45
Thermal	81	55
Torrance	66	47

RELATIVE HUMIDITY
High, 94%; low, 40%

TEMPERATURES & PRECIPITATION OVER THE FAR WEST

Station—	Max.	Min.	Precipitation
Albuquerque	68	31	....
Billings	63	37	....
Boise	66	36	....
Casper	51	31	....
Eureka	59	49	.54
Flagstaff	65	24	....
Great Falls	73	41	....
Helena	68	36	....
Las Vegas	77	47	....
Phoenix	82	52	....
Portland, Ore.	64	43	.05
Red Bluff	56	50	.28
Reno	71	26	....
Sacramento	69	45	....
Salt Lake City	63	38	.03
San Francisco	63	53	.02
Seattle	62	43	....
Spokane	65	35	.02
Tucson	77	47	....
Yuma	82	49	....

CANADIAN STATIONS

Station—	Max.	Min.	Precipitation
Montreal	50	36	....
Regina	59	36	....
Toronto	54	34	....
Vancouver	57	45	.32

Sun, Moon, Tide

NEW MOON	FIRST QUAR.	FULL MOON	LAST QUAR.
Apr. 29	May 7	Apr. 14	Apr. 21

THURSDAY, APRIL 8

Sun rises 5:30 a.m., sets 6:20 p.m.
Moon rises 12:17 a.m., sets 1:17 a.m.

April	High	low	high	low
8	3:20 4.1	10:44 0.3	•5:35 3.7	•10:47 2.2
9	4:37 4.4	11:29 0.1	•6:07 4.2	•11:45 1.5
10	5:42 4.7	12:11 0.1	•6:36 4.7	—
	Low	high	low	high
11	12:35 0.7	6:35 4.9	•12:51 0.1	•7:08 5.3

•Denotes p.m.

TEMPERATURES & PRECIPITATION OVER THE NATION

Station—	Max.	Min.	Precipitation
Albany	57	34	....
Amarillo	72	47	....
Anchorage	36	19	....
Asheville	71	31	....
Atlanta	76	46	....
Atlantic City	61	43	.02
Austin	75	61	.09
Baltimore	63	43	....
Birmingham	79	45	....
Bismarck	66	34	....
Boston	60	44	....
Brownsville	76	66	.95
Buffalo	49	31	....
Burlington, Vt.	42	23	....
Charleston, S.C.	74	57	....
Charleston, W.Va.	68	37	....
Charlotte, N.C.	73	41	....
Cheyenne	46	32	.15
Chicago	44	40	....
Cincinnati	69	41	....
Cleveland	53	31	....
Columbia, S.C.	81	40	....
Columbus, Oh.	62	31	....
Dallas-Ft. Worth	63	54	.43
Dayton	63	35	....
Denver	56	36	.01
Des Moines	64	52	....
Detroit	61	32	....
Duluth	44	28	....
El Paso	77	47	....
Fairbanks	38	20	....
Fargo	61	35	....
Hartford	58	42	.02
Honolulu	81	68	.02
Houston	73	57	.09
Indianapolis	67	40	....
Jackson, Miss.	79	44	....
Jacksonville	73	59	.05
Juneau	45	35	.07
Kansas City	75	50	....
Little Rock	75	53	....
Louisville	72	42	....
Memphis	78	49	....
Miami Beach	86	72	.35
Midlnd. Odessa	80	51	....
Milwaukee	48	38	....
Mpls.-St. Paul	62	42	....
Nashville	76	41	....
New Orleans	79	53	....
New York	59	42	....
Norfolk, Va.	64	47	....
North Platte	56	38	.04
Oklahoma City	70	56	.04
Omaha	58	51	.11
Orlando	81	65	.11
Philadelphia	62	41	....
Pittsburgh	58	34	....
Portland, Me.	52	30	....
Providence	55	43	....
Raleigh	73	40	....
Rapid City	49	32	.48
Richmond	71	43	....
St. Louis	75	43	....
St. Prbg. Tampa	79	64	.64
San Antonio	78	59	.06
St. Ste. Marie	37	24	....
Shreveport	80	45	....
Sioux Falls	65	49	.01
Syracuse	51	30	....
Tulsa	78	51	....
Washington	65	49	....
Wichita	75	53	.03

FOREIGN CITIES

City, Time	Weather	Temp.
Aberdeen, 1 p.m.	Ptly cldy	45
Amsterdam, 1 p.m.	Rain	39
Antigua, 8 a.m.	Cloudy	77
Athens, 2 p.m.	Ptly cldy	66
Auckland, mdnt.	Cloudy	64
Berlin, 1 p.m.	Cloudy	46
Beirut, 2 p.m.	Clear	66
Birmingham, 1 p.m.	Cloudy	43
Bonn, 1 p.m.	Cloudy	46
Brussels, 1 p.m.	Rain	48
Cairo, 2 p.m.	Clear	75
Casablanca, noon	Ptly cldy	61
Copenhagen, 1 p.m.	Ptly cldy	45
Dublin, 1 p.m.	Ptly cldy	48
Geneva, 1 p.m.	Rain	52
Guadalajara,	Clear	85
Hong Kong, 8 p.m.	Ptly cldy	66
Lisbon, Noon	Ptly cldy	57
London, 1 p.m.	Cloudy	52
Madrid, 1 p.m.	Clear	59
Malta, 1 p.m.	Clear	64
Manila, 8 p.m.	Clear	82
Mexico City,	Clear	79
Moscow, 3 p.m.	Cloudy	41
New Delhi, 5 p.m.	Clear	88
Nice, 1 p.m.	Clear	59
Oslo, 1 p.m.	Cloudy	48
Paris, 1 p.m.	Ptly cldy	52
Vienna, 1 p.m.	Cloudy	50
Warsaw, 1 p.m.	Clear	50

other ideas

A. Read weather forecasts in an almanac or watch weather reports on television. Plot the forecasts on a calendar. Compare forecasts with the actual daily weather.

B. Write and illustrate a book entitled "The Day the Big Rain. . . ."

C. Research why there are different types of weather.

D. Keep a monthly calendar of weather conditions in your area. At the end of the month, compute the percent of sunny days, rainy days, etc.

E. Predict tomorrow's weather. Justify your prediction.

F. Choose one of the following weather topics: hail, rain, sleet, snow, sun, wind. Think of ten words that could be used to describe your weather topic; for example, for *sun* you might list *sweltering, blistering, arid*, and the like. Illustrate your topic and add your words to the picture.

key words & phrases

forecast	pressure	showers	Celsius
mist	altitude	precipitation	extended forecast
humidity	arid	drizzle	Fahrenheit
circulate	tornado	static	torrent
stationary	drought	temperature	sweltering

self-evaluation

	date completed	possible score	your score	EXPERT	AVERAGE	FAIR	HELP!
1. Reading brief weather paragraph summaries		4					
2. Contrasting weather predictions for different localities within a state		8					
3. Locating weather information concerning different places in the country		13					
4. Interpreting symbols in weather reports		11					
5. Comparing national and international weather predictions		13					

CIRCLE **other ideas**
COMPLETED: A B C D E
                        F

TOTAL POSSIBLE POINTS: **49**

YOUR TOTAL POINTS:

How did you rate yourself?

name & date

From *Reading for Survival in Today's Society*, Volume One, ©1978 Goodyear Publishing Company, Inc.

driver's handbook

8

8

DRIVER'S HANDBOOK

Understanding a driver's handbook is more than a matter of memorizing the information needed to pass the driver's license examination. Knowledge of laws and facts cannot make careful drivers unless this knowledge is constantly applied in actual street-and-highway situations. This country's traffic statistics are grim proof that application does not automatically follow memorization. *In 1974, 30 billion dollars were lost as a result of traffic accidents.*[1] Yet, greater than the economic losses are the human losses, measured in injuries and fatalities, that result from auto accidents. As many as *one in every ten motor vehicles may be involved in an accident.*[2] From these statistics—and many more like them—it is obvious that the nation's drivers and potential drivers need to read driver education materials with greater skill and understanding.

Specific reading skills emphasized in this module are: (1) defining selected basic terms in driver education; (2) interpreting a point penalty system; (3) identifying highway signs; (4) reading paragraphs in a driver education handbook; and (5) understanding diagrams in driver's manuals.

materials

Encourage individual projects and group discussions to provide additional information related to operating an automobile. Make available copies of the driver's handbook used in your state.

[1]United States Bureau of the Census, *Statistical Abstract of the United States: 1975* (96th ed.; Washington, D.C.: U.S. Bureau of the Census, 1975), p. 577.
[2]Ibid.

survival reading skills

1. DEFINING SELECTED BASIC TERMS IN DRIVER EDUCATION

Use a copy of the driver's handbook or a dictionary if necessary to locate the meanings of these words as they apply to highway safety:

a. renewal license _____

_____

b. right-of-way _____

_____

c. interstate highway _____

_____

d. hazard _____

_____

e. emergency _____

_____

f. shoulder _____

_____

g. pedestrian _____

_____

h. median _____

_____

2. INTERPRETING A POINT PENALTY SYSTEM

Some states use a point penalty system for traffic violations. Read the explanation of **The Point System** and then the list of violations and points on page 78 Using the point system, compute J. Jones's points from this driving history:

January 11—ran a red light
February 1—ran a stop sign
February 6—drove 35 mph in a 25 mph zone
February 12—drove recklessly
February 19—drove 65 mph in a 55 mph zone

a. How many points does J. Jones have? _____

The Point System

Under the point system, violation points are assigned according to a statutory standard. Upon an accumulation of four violation points the Department is required to send the driver a letter of warning, and upon an accumulation of seven points the driver is afforded an opportunity to attend a conference with possible assignment to a driver improvement clinic. Completion of the course taught at the driver improvement clinic will result in three points being removed from his record. Suspensions under the point system are for a maximum of sixty days for a first suspension, for a maximum of six months for a second, and for a maximum of one year for a third. Restoration of a driver license following suspension under the point system and suspensions or revocations for any traffic violation cancels all previously assigned points on the driver's record.

As noted before, an accumulation of twelve points may result in the loss of your license, and driving while your license is suspended or revoked is a serious offense requiring a minimum fine of $200 or imprisonment for up to two years, or both.

THE NORTH CAROLINA POINT SYSTEM

Conviction	Point Value
Passing stopped school bus	5
Reckless driving	4
Hit and run, property damage only	4
Following too close	4
Driving on wrong side of road	4
Illegal passing	4
Running through stop sign	3
Speeding in excess of 55 miles an hour	3
Failing to yield right of way	3
Running through red light	3
No operator's license	3
Failure to stop for siren	3
Driving through safety zone	3
No liability insurance	3
Failure to report accident where such report is required	3
All other moving violations	2

b. What might happen to his license and to him? _____

_____

_____

c. How could he get three points removed? _____

_____

From *Reading for Survival in Today's Society*, Volume One, ©1978 Goodyear Publishing Company, Inc.

3. IDENTIFYING HIGHWAY SIGNS

On page 81 are two versions of the same **highway signs**. Read the existing sign in words and the new sign in symbols. On page 82 are symbol signs. In the space beside each symbol sign, write its meaning.

4. READING PARAGRAPHS IN A DRIVER EDUCATION HANDBOOK

The following questions relate to the five paragraphs from a **driver's handbook** (page 80). Locate the answer to each question, write the answer, and indicate by number whether the answer was found in the first, second, third, fourth, or fifth paragraph.

a. What must cars do until a blind pedestrian has crossed the intersection in front of the cars?_____

Answer found in paragraph_____.

b. Which should a pedestrian obey, special *walk* and *don't walk* signals or regular traffic signals? _____

_____

Answer found in paragraph_____.

c. Who has the right-of-way at an intersection where the crosswalk is marked and there is no traffic signal, automobiles or pedestrians? _____

_____

Answer found in paragraph_____.

d. If a pedestrian is in the street and the traffic light turns to yellow or red, what must drivers do? _____

Answer found in paragraph_____.

5. UNDERSTANDING DIAGRAMS IN DRIVER'S MANUALS

Complete the following by reading information in the **diagram** on page 80.

a. If a car is traveling 50 mph, it takes _____ feet to stop the car.

b. If a car is traveling 30 mph, it takes _____ feet to stop the car.

c. If a car is traveling 60 mph, it will go _____ feet before the driver can apply brakes and _____ feet before it stops.

PEDESTRIANS

Because of his low speed and lack of defensive armor, the pedestrian is a poor match for the automobile. In cities, one out of every three people killed in auto accidents is a pedestrian; in rural areas, one out of every five. Most of the pedestrians killed are children and elderly persons.

THE DRIVER AND THE PEDESTRIAN

At an intersection with no traffic signal, pedestrians have the right-of-way if they are in marked crosswalks, or in unmarked crosswalks formed by imagining the sidewalks to continue across the streets. Pedestrians also have the right-of-way at marked crosswalks in the middle of a city block or in the open country.

The law entitles a blind pedestrian to special consideration at intersections where there are no traffic signals. If a blind pedestrian holds out a white cane or a white cane tipped with red, or if he is accompanied by a guide dog, all cars approaching the intersection must come to a full stop. They must remain stopped until the blind pedestrian has completed his crossing.

At intersections controlled by ordinary traffic signals, pedestrians must obey the same signals as drivers going in the same direction. They may not start to cross on a red or yellow light. When crossing on a green light, they have the right-of-way over all vehicles, including those turning across the path of the pedestrian. If a light changes to yellow or red while a pedestrian is still in the street, drivers must allow him to complete his crossing safely.

At some intersections, special signals instruct pedestrians either to walk or don't walk. Where these are in operation, pedestrians must obey them instead of the regular traffic signals. Pedestrians crossing on a special pedestrian signal have the right-of-way just as they do when crossing on a green light.

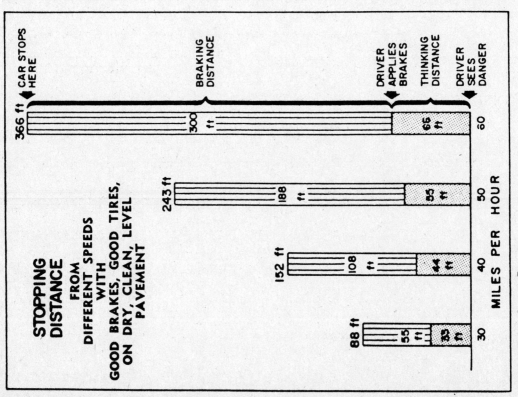

STOPPING DISTANCE
FROM DIFFERENT SPEEDS WITH
GOOD BRAKES, GOOD TIRES, ON DRY, CLEAN, LEVEL PAVEMENT

CAR STOPS HERE

366 ft

300 ft

BRAKING DISTANCE

DRIVER APPLIES BRAKES

THINKING DISTANCE

DRIVER SEES DANGER

65 ft

60

243 ft

188 ft

55 ft

50

152 ft

108 ft

44 ft

40

88 ft

55 ft

33 ft

30

MILES PER HOUR

National Safety Council Figures

From *Reading for Survival in Today's Society, Volume One*, © 1978 Goodyear Publishing Company, Inc.

From *Reading for Survival in Today's Society*, Volume One, ©1978 Goodyear Publishing Company, Inc.

EXISTING	NEW	EXISTING	NEW	EXISTING	NEW
DIVIDED HIGHWAY		SLIPPERY WHEN WET		SIGNAL AHEAD	
DIVIDED HIGHWAY ENDS		PEDESTRIAN CROSSING		MERGING TRAFFIC	
YIELD	YIELD	LOW CLEARANCE 12 FT 6 IN	12'-6"	TWO WAY TRAFFIC	
NO RIGHT TURN		KEEP RIGHT		SCHOOL	
NO U TURN		DO NOT ENTER	DO NOT ENTER	HILL	
DEER CROSSING		NO TRUCKS		DO NOT PASS WHEN YELLOW LINE IS IN YOUR LANE	DO NOT PASS WHEN SOLID YELLOW LINE IS IN YOUR LANE

82

other ideas

A. Select one topic in the driver's handbook. Read and discuss additional information concerning that topic.

B. Collect and bring to class newspaper accounts of traffic accidents during a one-week period. Collect other kinds of information related to automobile use, such as articles concerning highway construction and classified advertisements of autos for sale.

C. Observe actual driving practices. If possible, watch a particular intersection during rush hours. Note instances in which traffic regulations are repeatedly observed or violated. Discuss possible causes and consequences of violations and what might be done to reduce or eliminate them.

D. Role play a scene in which a driver is in court as a result of a traffic violation or a series of violations.

E. Using the driver's manual of your state, make out a test to be taken by your friends.

F. Trace briefly the history of driver licensing.

G. Using the library, discover if other countries require the operators of vehicles to have licenses.

H. Paste road or traffic signs on small cards. In turn each player selects a card, tells the meaning of the sign, and advances one space on a racetrack diagram or other game board. If the player cannot identify the sign, he or she does not advance. To add variety, include bonus and penalty cards, such as:

OUT OF GAS
GO BACK 1 SPACE

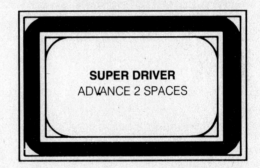

SUPER DRIVER
ADVANCE 2 SPACES

key words & phrases

vehicle	steer	hazard	parallel
curve	collision	shoulder	intersection
examiner	signal	upgrade	accelerate
skid	crosswalk	reverse	violation
siren	motorist	illegal	right-of-way

self-evaluation

	date completed	possible score	your score	EXPERT	AVERAGE	FAIR	HELP!
1. Defining selected basic terms in driver education		8					
2. Interpreting a point penalty system		3					
3. Identifying highway signs		18					
4. Reading paragraphs in a driver education handbook		8					
5. Understanding diagrams in driver's manuals		4					

CIRCLE **other ideas**
COMPLETED: A B C D E
          F G H

TOTAL POSSIBLE POINTS:
41

YOUR TOTAL POINTS:

How did you rate yourself?

name & date

_____

signs

9

SIGNS

Within the past decade, an increasing number of signs have appeared beside streets and highways, in stores, in public transportation terminals, and in homes. Signs can be used to picture or state intended uses, identify locations, indicate distances, give directions, list hours and conditions of operation, or give warnings. Signs ranging from simple ON-OFF labels on light switches to complicated operation directions on kitchen appliances and intricate computer announcements of airline flights have become an integral part of our lives. Although many signs employ both words and symbols to convey their messages, the current trend is toward deleting words from signs, partly because a large number of persons are unable to read even the most common words. Signs with and without words are included in this module.

Specific reading skills emphasized in this module are: (1) understanding location signs; (2) reading European picture signs; (3) interpreting identification signs; (4) identifying directional signs; and (5) recognizing warning signs.

materials

In addition to this module's illustrations of a variety of signs, students should make and bring to class drawings of different signs they encounter during a specified period of time.

survival reading skills

1. UNDERSTANDING LOCATION SIGNS

Beside each of the **location signs** on page 88 is an alphabet letter. On the line following each question below, write the letter that identifies the appropriate sign.

a. Which sign would *not* be found beside a street or highway?_____

b. Which sign gives distances to specified destinations? _____

c. Which signs tell what street or road to use to visit a vacation spot?

_____ and _____

d. Which sign was probably written by hand?_____

e. Which sign would be found inside a place? _____

f. Which direction would you travel to go to the camera shop? (You are facing the drugstore.) _____

_____

g. Which direction would you travel to go to the men's clothing store?_____

_____

h. If you went to the right, how many stores would you pass before getting to the cafeteria?_____

2. READING EUROPEAN PICTURE SIGNS

Because of the great variety of languages spoken in Europe, it has become common practice there to use signs without words. These picture signs are also becoming popular in the United States. Look at the six **European picture signs** on page 89 and write a possible meaning for each one on the lines below.

a. _____

b. _____

c. _____

d. _____

e. _____

f. _____

location signs

A

B

C

D

WINONA   27 km

COLUMBUS   153 km

E

European picture signs

3. INTERPRETING IDENTIFICATION SIGNS

Beside each **identification sign** is an alphabet letter. On the line following each question below, write the appropriate letter.

a. Which sign is the most common type? _____

b. Which sign would be found in a grocery store? _____

c. Which sign would be found in an airport? _____

d. Which sign would probably be found at a large meeting? _____

e. What hours is the store open

   (1) on Wednesday? _____

   (2) on Saturday? _____

   (3) on Sunday? _____

identification signs

A

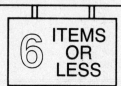

C

E

B

store hours	
M-F:	9 to 9
SAT:	9 to 6
SUN:	1 to 6

D

From *Reading for Survival in Today's Society,* Volume One, ©1978, Goodyear Publishing Company, Inc.

directional signs

push	pull

A

ENTRANCE	EXIT

B

OPEN	CLOSE

C

IN	OUT

D

escalator   escalator

E

4. IDENTIFYING DIRECTIONAL SIGNS

Beside each pair of **directional signs** is an alphabet letter. Write the appropriate letter on the line following each question below.

a. Which two pairs of signs might you find on a washing machine?

(1) _____

(2) _____

b. Which two pairs of signs might you find in a two-story furniture building?

(1) _____

(2) _____

c. Which two pairs of signs might you find in a cafeteria line?

(1) _____

(2) _____

d. Which pair of signs might you find on a cereal box? _____

5. RECOGNIZING WARNING SIGNS

Beside each **warning sign** is an alphabet letter. Complete each question below by writing the correct letter in the blank.

a. There are at least two signs that should be observed by joggers. What

are they? _____ and _____

b. Which sign would probably be found on a house, gate, or fence? _____

c. Which sign might be on a large truck carrying an explosive, such as

gasoline? _____

d. Which three signs warn certain people to "stay away" from this property?

_____, _____, and _____

---

warning signs

A

DANGER
FLAMMABLE LIQUID
B

Beware
of
Dog
C

NO
SMOKING
D

bird sanctuary
NO
HUNTING
E

NO TRESPASSING
F

From *Reading for Survival in Today's Society*, Volume One, ©1978 Goodyear Publishing Company, Inc.

other ideas

A. Make a booklet of signs you have designed to give people basic information about a topic, such as shopping, safety, or traveling.

B. Select one area or topic, such as streets, shopping centers, public transportation terminals, or kitchen appliances. Collect information about signs posted in your area or related to your topic. You may want to take notes, make sketches, take photographs, or cut pictures from magazines on brochures. Discuss the meaning of each sign. Use your signs to make a collage.

C. Using **identification signs** C, D, and E on page 90, write a story about a person in a grocery store. The signs should play an important part in the story.

D. Design signs to be used in your classroom or school. With the principal's and teacher's permission, post them where appropriate.

E. Make a list of all the signs you see on your way home.

F. On 2″ x 3″ cards, paste various road directional and locational symbol or picture signs. On another set of cards, write the word for which the symbol stands. Play Concentration. The winner is the student who successfully matches the most words and signs.

G. Paste various signs on one side of a pizza disk. Beside or under each sign, make a hole. On the other side of the disk, beside or under the hole, write the words for which the sign stands. Place or hold the pizza disk so that you can see the signs and your partner can see their meanings. Put a pencil in the hole beside or under one of the signs. Tell what the sign means. Ask your partner to check your answers. Trade places with your partner or turn the disk around.

H. Create a story using pictures or signs in place of key words. Exchange stories with a friend and each read the other's story.

key words & phrases

exit	posted	beware	loading zone
vacancy	manager	elevator	deer crossing
entrance	no hunting	high voltage	pedestrian
escalator	one way	trespassing	garage sale
sale	loiter	danger	for rent

self-evaluation

	date completed	possible score	your score	EXPERT	AVERAGE	FAIR	HELP!
1. Understanding location signs		9					
2. Reading European travel signs		6					
3. Interpreting identification signs		7					
4. Identifying directional signs		7					
5. Recognizing warning signs		7					

CIRCLE **other ideas**
COMPLETED: A B C D E
       F G H

TOTAL POSSIBLE POINTS: **36**

YOUR TOTAL POINTS:

How did you rate yourself?

name & date

_____

maps

10

10

MAPS

Maps encountered outside school differ markedly in appearance and content from most of those found in textbooks. After all, most of us have a far greater need to find our way to and around unfamiliar spots (for example, shopping centers, school campuses, or tourist attractions) and to understand time zone changes and bus, train, or plane routes than to locate the Tropic of Cancer or the Prime Meridian. Because of the increased amount of travel by Americans, both within the community and in larger geographical areas, students need to be able to read different kinds of maps. *The key to efficient use of any map is understanding its legend and its purpose.*

Specific reading lessons emphasized in this module are: (1) using top and side symbols to locate buildings on a map; (2) determining various routes to one location; (3) finding convenient accommodations; (4) reading street names on a map; and (5) locating time zones on a map.

materials

In addition to the different maps included in this module, suggest students collect and bring to class a variety of maps—road, city, building, shopping center, state, national, world, blueprints, and floor plans.

survival reading skills

1. USING TOP AND SIDE SYMBOLS TO LOCATE BUILDINGS ON A MAP

Use the lower right part of the **Duke University Campus Map** to find the names of the buildings listed below. Then, use the numbers down the side of the map and the letters across the top to locate the building. When you find the building, circle it. The number-letter designation in parentheses beside the name of the building on the lower right part of the map tells you where on the map to look for the building. Write the number-letter beside the name of each building below.

a. Wade Stadium _____

b. Duke Hospital _____

c. Art Museum _____

d. West Duke Building _____

e. Perkins Library _____

2. DETERMINING VARIOUS ROUTES TO ONE LOCATION

a. If you were traveling to the campus illustrated on the **Main Routes to the Campus** map *from* each of the following places, which highway would you use?

(1) Greensboro?   Highway _____

(2) Richmond?   Highway _____

(3) Raleigh?   Highway _____

(4) Chapel Hill?   Highway _____

b. Some roads and streets have both a name and a numerical designation. What number is assigned to each of the following roads?

(1) Hope Valley Road?   Highway _____

(2) Roxboro Road?   Highway _____

(3) Alston Avenue?   Highway _____

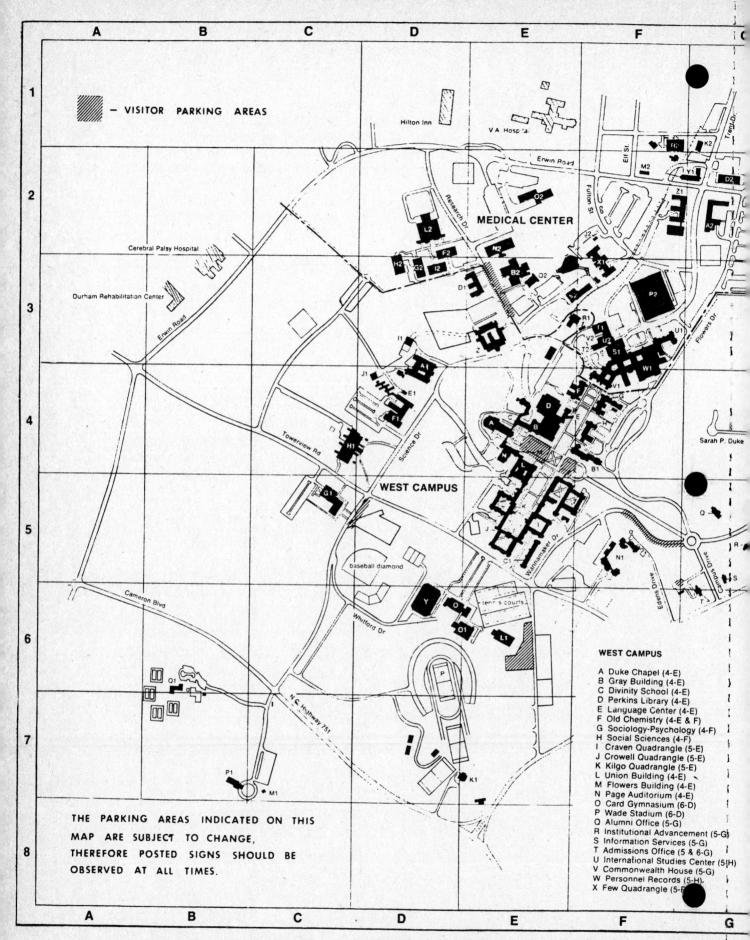

- VISITOR PARKING AREAS

Hilton Inn

V A Hosp 'a'

Erwin Road

Elf St.

K2

M2

D2

Research Dr.

MEDICAL CENTER

Fulton St.

Y1

Z1

A2

Cerebral Palsy Hospital

O2

L2

J2

X1

Durham Rehabilitation Center

H2 G2 I2

F2

N2

B2 O2

D1

P2

Flowers Dr.

Erwin Road

R1

U1

I1

V2

U3

T2

S1

W1

Z

V1

G

A1

J1

E1

D

A C

E

H

F1

Sarah P. Duke

Towerview Rd.

H1

B

B1

Science Dr.

G1

WEST CAMPUS

Q

J

K

I

N1

R

baseball diamond

C1

Wannamaker Dr.

Eden's Drive

Campus Drive

T

S

Cameron Blvd

Y

O

tennis courts

Whitford Dr.

O1

L1

O1

P

N.C. Highway 751

WEST CAMPUS

A Duke Chapel (4-E)
B Gray Building (4-E)
C Divinity School (4-E)
D Perkins Library (4-E)
E Language Center (4-E)
F Old Chemistry (4-E & F)
G Sociology-Psychology (4-F)
H Social Sciences (4-F)
I Craven Quadrangle (5-E)
J Crowell Quadrangle (5-E)
K Kilgo Quadrangle (5-E)
L Union Building (4-E)
M Flowers Building (4-E)
N Page Auditorium (4-E)
O Card Gymnasium (6-D)
P Wade Stadium (6-D)
Q Alumni Office (5-G)
R Institutional Advancement (5-G)
S Information Services (5-G)
T Admissions Office (5 & 6-G)
U International Studies Center (5-H)
V Commonwealth House (5-G)
W Personnel Records (5-H)
X Few Quadrangle (5-E)

P1

M1

THE PARKING AREAS INDICATED ON THIS
MAP ARE SUBJECT TO CHANGE,
THEREFORE POSTED SIGNS SHOULD BE
OBSERVED AT ALL TIMES.

K1

DUKE UNIVERSITY CAMPUS MAP

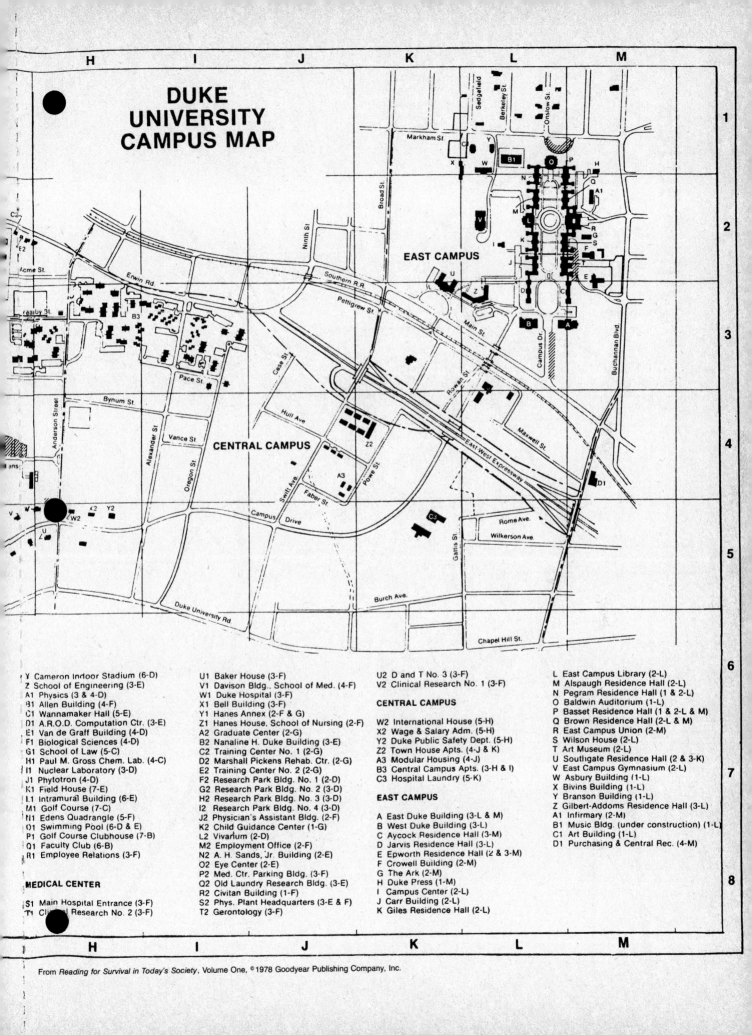

EAST CAMPUS

CENTRAL CAMPUS

Y Cameron Indoor Stadium (6-D)
Z School of Engineering (3-E)
A1 Physics (3 & 4-D)
B1 Allen Building (4-F)
C1 Wannamaker Hall (5-E)
D1 A.R.O.D. Computation Ctr. (3-E)
E1 Van de Graff Building (4-D)
F1 Biological Sciences (4-D)
G1 School of Law (5-C)
H1 Paul M. Gross Chem. Lab. (4-C)
I1 Nuclear Laboratory (3-D)
J1 Phytotron (4-D)
K1 Field House (7-E)
L1 Intramural Building (6-E)
M1 Golf Course (7-C)
N1 Edens Quadrangle (5-F)
O1 Swimming Pool (6-D & E)
P1 Golf Course Clubhouse (7-B)
Q1 Faculty Club (6-B)
R1 Employee Relations (3-F)

MEDICAL CENTER

S1 Main Hospital Entrance (3-F)
T1 Clinical Research No. 2 (3-F)

U1 Baker House (3-F)
V1 Davison Bldg., School of Med. (4-F)
W1 Duke Hospital (3-F)
X1 Bell Building (3-F)
Y1 Hanes Annex (2-F & G)
Z1 Hanes House, School of Nursing (2-F)
A2 Graduate Center (2-G)
B2 Nanaline H. Duke Building (3-E)
C2 Training Center No. 1 (2-G)
D2 Marshall Pickens Rehab. Ctr. (2-G)
E2 Training Center No. 2 (2-G)
F2 Research Park Bldg. No. 1 (2-D)
G2 Research Park Bldg. No. 2 (3-D)
H2 Research Park Bldg. No. 3 (3-D)
I2 Research Park Bldg. No. 4 (3-D)
J2 Physician's Assistant Bldg. (2-F)
K2 Child Guidance Center (1-G)
L2 Vivarium (2-D)
M2 Employment Office (2-F)
N2 A. H. Sands, Jr. Building (2-E)
O2 Eye Center (2-E)
P2 Med. Ctr. Parking Bldg. (3-F)
Q2 Old Laundry Research Bldg. (3-E)
R2 Civitan Building (1-F)
S2 Phys. Plant Headquarters (3-E & F)
T2 Gerontology (3-F)

U2 D and T No. 3 (3-F)
V2 Clinical Research No. 1 (3-F)

CENTRAL CAMPUS

W2 International House (5-H)
X2 Wage & Salary Adm. (5-H)
Y2 Duke Public Safety Dept. (5-H)
Z2 Town House Apts. (4-J & K)
A3 Modular Housing (4-J)
B3 Central Campus Apts. (3-H & I)
C3 Hospital Laundry (5-K)

EAST CAMPUS

A East Duke Building (3-L & M)
B West Duke Building (3-L)
C Aycock Residence Hall (3-M)
D Jarvis Residence Hall (3-L)
E Epworth Residence Hall (2 & 3-M)
F Crowell Building (2-M)
G The Ark (2-M)
H Duke Press (1-M)
I Campus Center (2-L)
J Carr Building (2-L)
K Giles Residence Hall (2-L)

L East Campus Library (2-L)
M Alspaugh Residence Hall (2-L)
N Pegram Residence Hall (1 & 2-L)
O Baldwin Auditorium (1-L)
P Basset Residence Hall (1 & 2-L & M)
Q Brown Residence Hall (2-L & M)
R East Campus Union (2-M)
S Wilson House (2-L)
T Art Museum (2-L)
U Southgate Residence Hall (2 & 3-K)
V East Campus Gymnasium (2-L)
W Asbury Building (1-L)
X Bivins Building (1-L)
Y Branson Building (1-L)
Z Gilbert-Addoms Residence Hall (3-L)
A1 Infirmary (2-M)
B1 Music Bldg. (under construction) (1-L)
C1 Art Building (1-L)
D1 Purchasing & Central Rec. (4-M)

From *Reading for Survival in Today's Society*, Volume One, ©1978 Goodyear Publishing Company, Inc.

MAIN ROUTES TO THE CAMPUS

TO RICHMOND

15

I-85

TO GREENSBORO

I-85 70

HILLSBORO RD.

DUKE FOREST

ROXBORO RD.

501

BYPASS

GEER ST.

MARKHAM AVE.

MAGNUM ST.

DUKE ST.

GREGSON ST.

MAIN ST.

BUCHANAN BLVD.

MILTON

MARKHAM AVE.

DUKE ST.

GUESS RD.

BROAD ST.

GUESS RD.

70

BYPASS

15-501

ERWIN RD.

MORREENE RD.

SWIFT AVE.

CAMPUS DR.

DUKE UNIVERSITY RD.

ANDERSON ST.

KENT ST.

CHAPEL HILL ST.

ROXBORO ST.

ELIZABETH

RAMSEUR

E. PEABODY

PETTIGREW

ALSTON AVE.

DRIVER

BRIGGS AVE.

WAKE FOREST RD.

98

TO RALEIGH, AIRPORT
NORTH CAROLINA STATE UNIVERSITY

70

I-40

NORTH CAROLINA CENTRAL UNIVERSITY

FAYETTEVILLE ST.

CHAPEL HILL RD.

CHAPEL HILL BLVD.

CORNWALLIS RD.

UNIVERSITY DR.

HOPE VALLEY RD.

55

TO RESEARCH TRIANGLE

751

751

PINECREST RD.

751

CORNWALLIS RD.

SHANNON RD.

GARRETT RD.

BYPASS

751

TO CHAPEL HILL,
UNIVERSITY OF NORTH CAROLINA

15-50

OLD CHAPEL HILL RD.

Mt. Morah Church Rd.

Weaver Dairy Rd

Booker Creek

1. Tower View Rd.
2. Science Dr.
3. Hospital Dr.
4. Trent Dr.
5. Yearby Ave.
6. Flowers Dr.
7. Wannamaker Dr
8. Campus Dr.

From *Reading for Survival in Today's Society*, Volume One. ©1978 Goodyear Publishing Company, Inc.

From *Reading for Survival in Today's Society*, Volume One. ©1978 Goodyear Publishing Company, Inc.

3. FINDING CONVENIENT ACCOMMODATIONS

Maps such as the **Map and Accommodations Directory** on pages 102 and 103 would be most useful when you found yourself in a new city. Two major features of this map should be noted: (1) numbers on the map indicate points of interest in the city, and (2) letters on the map designate motels/hotels. Use this map to answer the following questions:

a. What is the nearest motel/hotel to the Morehead Planetarium and

Observatory? _____

_____

b. What is the nearest motel/hotel to the North Carolina Museum of Life and

Science? _____

_____

c. What are the two nearest motels/hotels to the Research Triangle Park?

(1) _____

(2) _____

d. What are the names of two streets close to the Ramada Inn–Downtown?

(1) _____

(2) _____

e. What are the names of two streets near North Carolina Central University?

(1) _____

(2) _____

4. READING STREET NAMES ON A MAP

Locate the answers to each of the following by reading information on the **Map and Accommodations Directory** on pages 102 and 103.

a. If you travel east on Hillsborough Road, it becomes _____

_____ Avenue.

b. If you travel west on Cornwallis Road, you cross which North Carolina

road? _____

From *Reading for Survival in Today's Society*, Volume One,
© 1978 Goodyear Publishing Company, Inc.

c. If you travel west on Holloway Street, it first becomes _____

_____ Street, and then it is

called _____ Road.

d. If you travel south from the northernmost part of Guess Road, the first

street you cross on the map is _____

e. The northernmost street named on this map is _____

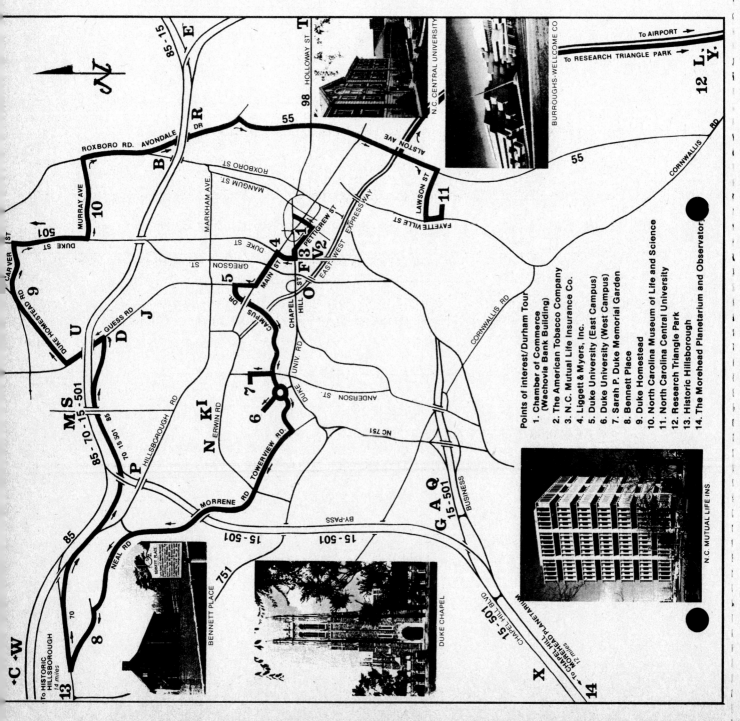

Points of interest/Durham Tour
1. Chamber of Commerce (Wachovia Bank Building)
2. The American Tobacco Company
3. N.C. Mutual Life Insurance Co.
4. Liggett & Myers, Inc.
5. Duke University (East Campus)
6. Duke University (West Campus)
7. Sarah P. Duke Memorial Garden
8. Bennett Place
9. Duke Homestead
10. North Carolina Museum of Life and Science
11. North Carolina Central University
12. Research Triangle Park
13. Historic Hillsborough
14. The Morehead Planetarium and Observatory

Accommodations Directory

Hotel/Motel Name Address	Map Location	Phone	Guest Rooms	Meeting Rooms, Capacity	Facilities
Carolina Duke Motor Inn 2517 Guess Road	D	286-0771	99		SP, R nearby
Cavalier Inn Durham-Chapel Hill Blvd.	A	489-9122	60		SP, R nearby
Chesterfield Motel I-85 at Roxboro Road	B	477-7343	44		R nearby
Confederate Inn I-85 at U.S. 70 West	C	383-2561	43		SP, R nearby
The Cricket Inn I-05 at Hillandale Road	M	383-2549	120		SP, R nearby
Days Inn I-85 at Redwood Road	E	688-4338	120		R, SP
Downtowner Motor Inn 309 W. Chapel Hill Street	F	688-8221	156	1 to 4 rooms, 10 to 375 persons	R, SP, GP
Duke Motor Lodge Durham-Chapel Hill Blvd.	G	489-9111	76	1 room, 15 persons	SP, R nearby
Dutch Village Motel 2306 Elder Street	I	286-7788	54		R, K
Econo-Travel Motor Lodge 2337 Guess Road	J	286-7746	48		SP
El Rancho Motel Erwin Road at Elf St.	K	286-4421	18		R nearby
Governors Inn I-40 at Davis Drive	L	549-8631	128	1 to 7 rooms, 10 to 400 persons	R, SP, GP
Happy Inn I-85 at Avondale Drive	R	683-1321	145		SP, R nearby, GP
Hilton Inn 2424 Erwin Road	N	286-7761	135	1 to 4 rooms, 15 to 75 persons	R, SP, GP
Holiday Inn-West US 15-501 at US 70 West	P	383-1551	143	1 to 6 rooms, 10 to 300 persons	R,SP, GP
Homestead Motel Durham-Chapel Hill Blvd.	Q	489-9181	24		R nearby
Howard Johnson's Motor Lodge I-85 at Hillandale Road	S	477-7381	80	1 room, 75 persons	R, SP
Motel 6 2101 Holloway Street	T	682-8043	121		SP, R nearby
Ramada Inn I-85 at Guess Road	U	477-7371	100	1 to 4 rooms, 25 to 300 persons	R, SP
Ramada Inn — Downtown East-West Expway at Duke St.	V	683-1531	159	1 to 4 rooms, 10 to 250 persons	R, SP, GP
Skyland Motel I-85 at US 70 West	W	383-2508	31		SP, R nearby
Sleepy Time Inn Durham-Chapel Hill Blvd.	X	489-9146	76		R, SP
Triangle Motel Raleigh-Durham Airport	Y	596-6218	78	1 room, 30 persons	SP, R nearby
Washington Duke Motor Inn 605 W. Chapel Hill Street	O	682-5411	131	1 to 2 rooms, 20 to 200 persons	R, SP, GP

Code: R-restaurant   SP-swimming pool   GP-golf privileges   K-kitchenettes
All Hotels/Motels have television, parking, air conditioning and telephones.

From *Reading for Survival in Today's Society*, Volume One, ©1978 Goodyear Publishing Company, Inc.

5. LOCATING TIME ZONES ON A MAP
Refer to the **United Airlines** map on page 105 and write which time zone each of the following is in:

a. Bakersfield, California _____

b. Charleston, West Virginia _____

c. Fort Lauderdale, Florida _____

d. Boston, Massachusetts _____

e. Vancouver, British Columbia_____

f. Kansas City, Missouri _____

g. Des Moines, Iowa_____

h. Cleveland, Ohio _____

i. Salem, Oregon _____

other ideas

A. On a small section of a state or local map, locate and circle one or more key symbols identified in the map's legend. Discuss the meaning of each of the symbols.

B. Compare a city, a state, and a national map. List similar symbols used on all three.

C. Locate your home and school on a city map. Trace the shortest route between the two places. Compute the approximate distance by using the map mileage legend.

D. Use a world map to play Twenty Questions. Select a mystery vacation spot. Your partner must find his way there by analyzing your answers to a series of twenty questions he poses. For example, he might ask:
Is it located within 50 miles of an ocean?
Is its population over 50,000?
Vary the game by giving clues rather than having your partner ask questions.

E. Mark cities visited by students in your class on a United States map with colored pins. Using the map legend, compute the distances traveled.

F. Play "I'm Thinking of a State (or Country)" by using a United States or world map. Questioners should ask *directional* questions only, such as "Is it *north* of Iowa?"

G. In any module in which a location is mentioned, find that place on a map. For example, if completing a Social Security form, find the general location of the Social Security office on a city map. If completing a credit card application form, find on a map the location of the city to which the form is to be mailed.

From *Reading for Survival in Today's Society, Volume One*, ©1978 Goodyear Publishing Company, Inc.

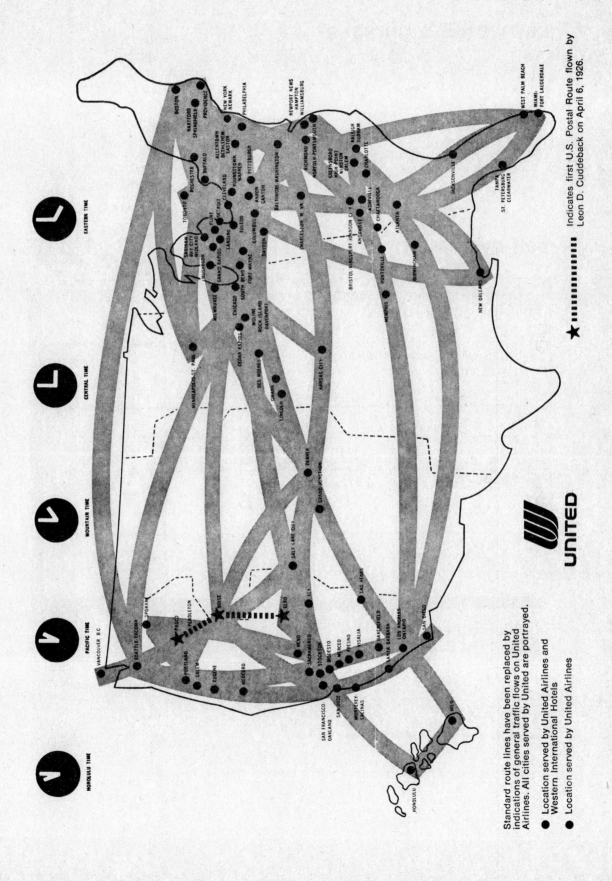

key words & phrases

cape	route	channel	toll road
banks	key	canal	peninsula
desert	inlet	republic	equator
swamp	island	sound	interstate
port	strait	detour	primary road

self-evaluation

	date completed	possible score	your score	EXPERT	AVERAGE	FAIR	HELP!
1. Using top and side symbols to locate buildings on a map		10					
2. Determining various routes to one location		7					
3. Finding convenient accommodations		8					
4. Reading street names on a map		6					
5. Locating time zones on a map		9					

CIRCLE **other ideas**
COMPLETED: A B C D E
F G

TOTAL POSSIBLE POINTS: **40**

YOUR TOTAL POINTS:

How did you rate yourself?

name & date

From *Reading for Survival in Today's Society*, Volume One, ©1978 Goodyear Publishing Company, Inc.

travel
information

11

11

TRAVEL INFORMATION

Travel—whether for business or pleasure—is big business. In 1974, over 8½ billion dollars were spent by overseas travelers with an average expenditure per day of $22.58.[1] It is estimated that *Americans travel over one trillion road miles per year,*[2] *and spend over 48 billion dollars on vacations alone!*[3]

When planning a major trip, many persons consult travel agencies and request free or inexpensive travel brochures. Others become intrigued with travel information received in the mail or found in magazines, newspapers, or travel books. Careful reading of this information usually helps them choose routes, stopovers, and destination, or plan a tour itinerary. Students should learn where to obtain travel information and how to interpret it.

Specific reading lessons emphasized in this module are: (1) identifying special features in a vacation description; (2) distinguishing between fact and opinion in travel literature; (3) comparing hotel costs in one geographical area; (4) comparing hotel costs in two different cities; and (5) finding and interpreting details in travel brochures.

materials

Suggest students collect and bring to class a variety of brochures describing different types of transportation, geographical locations, and major tourist attractions. Post clippings from travel magazines and newspapers on the class bulletin board.

[1]United States Bureau of the Census, *Statistical Abstract of the United States: 1975* (96th ed.; Washington, D.C.: U.S. Bureau of the Census, 1975), p. 219.

[2]Ann Golenpaul, ed., *Information Please Almanac, Atlas and Yearbook 1975* (29th ed.; New York: Simon & Schuster, 1975), p. ii.

[3]Ibid., p. 62.

survival reading skills

1. IDENTIFYING SPECIAL FEATURES IN A VACATION DESCRIPTION

Refer to the **"Tennis and Golf in Puerto Rico"** information and answer the following questions:

a. How many days and nights does the price cover? _____

_____

b. Is there an additional charge for golf and tennis? _____

c. What is the difference between accommodations for double occupancy

and for triple occupancy? _____

_____

d. What kind of transportation is provided in the charge? _____

_____

_____

e. What would it cost you to use this transportation? _____

_____

f. Does the $50.00 include air fare? _____

Tennis and Golf in Puerto Rico
$50.00*

4 DAYS/3 NIGHTS

Palmas Del Mar

Double Occupancy Features
- Accommodation with terrace.
- Unlimited greens fees and tennis for entire stay.
- Sub-compact automatic shift car for three 24 hour periods plus 15¢ per mile. (Air conditioning, Collision Damage Waiver and gasoline extra.)

Triple Occupancy Features
- Accommodations in suite.
- Same features as double occupancy features listed above.

PER PERSON RATES Effective: through Dec. 15, 1975. **European Plan.**

Double	Extra Night	Triple	Extra Night
$50.00	$18.50	$50.00	$15.50

IT5EA1FFOA/IT5EA1WPDM

• **Per person, double occupancy, air fare additional.**

Minimum age 21 years for car rental.

2. **DISTINGUISHING BETWEEN FACT AND OPINION IN TRAVEL LITERATURE**

Refer to the **"Lock Up and Go"** advertisement.

a. Read each of the phrases below. Consider how it is used in the advertisement. On the line following the phrase, write *fact* or *opinion*, depending on which you feel it is.

(1) Autumn Weekenders for you in Miami Beach, Ft. Lauderdale or Key

Biscayne _____

(2) give you a great time _____

(3) charge it all on Wings® _____

(4) leave it all behind_____

(5) a weekend that won't take weeks to pay for_____

b. Discuss how each of these phrases might be interpreted differently, depending on how persons react to them.

Lock up and go:

For a weekend that won't take you weeks to pay for.

Leave it all behind.

Forget about raking the leaves, they'll be there when you get back. Put off cleaning up the garage and ordering firewood.

It can wait.

Instead, get away for a weekend that'll cost just about what it does to stay home, but will do you a lot more good. A weekend that won't take weeks to pay for.

We've put together a group of Autumn Weekenders for you in Miami Beach, Ft. Lauderdale or Key Biscayne. In Puerto Rico, or Daytona Beach.

Getting away for three or four days makes all the difference how you feel when you get back. You don't even mind those chores.

Without too much planning or packing, you can be out of your old weekend routine and into some new pleasures. And we've gone out of our way to pack in some extras you won't find elsewhere.

Eastern's Autumn Weekenders take you there at low cost, give you a great time, and get you home relaxed and ready for winter. And to make it even more relaxing, you can charge it all on Wings,® Eastern's personal credit card, American Express, Master Charge, Bank Americard, or any other major credit card.

Decide where you'd enjoy next weekend most. Then call the travel specialist, your Travel Agent, or Eastern.

And lock the front door.

From *Reading for Survival in Today's Society,* Volume One, ©1978 Goodyear Publishing Company, Inc.

3. COMPARING HOTEL COSTS IN ONE GEOGRAPHICAL AREA
Refer to the **"Leave It All Behind for Walt Disney World"** advertisement
and answer the following questions:

a. Which is the most expensive for a double room, Rodeway Inn or Hilton

Inn South? _____

b. Which hotel charges the least amount to spend an extra night in a double

room? _____

c. Which is the most expensive hotel for a single room?_____

_____

d. Which is the least expensive hotel for a single room?_____

_____

e. If one family stayed in a triple room at the Hyatt of Orlando and another
family stayed in a triple room at Travelodge International, what would be

the total cost of the rooms?_____

f. Is there a charge for a ten-year-old child sharing a room with his or her

parents?_____

g. What would be the added charge to your double room if you rented a full

size sedan for one day? $_____

4. COMPARING HOTEL COSTS IN TWO DIFFERENT CITIES
Compare the information described for the vacation on the **Florida Gulf
Coast** and the vacation at **Daytona Beach** and answer the following:

a. In which city could you get the least expensive double room? _____

_____

b. In which city and at which hotel can you rent a one-bedroom apartment?

(1) City_____

(2) Hotel_____

c. What is the time period for the rates described for the Ramada Inn

South?_____

Leave it all behind for Walt Disney World.
Only $48⁵⁰–$77⁰⁰

No charge for children under 11 sharing room with parents.
Features charge for children:
Ages 3-11, car $11.00; transfers $16.75.
Ages 12-17, car $12.00; transfers $21.50.

*Rates quoted are for transfer plan. If selecting car plan, add $13.00 single; $6.50 double; and $4.33 triple for each adult. Intermediate cars are available for an additional $2.00 per day single; $1.00 per day double; and $.67 per day triple. Full size sedans—$4.00 per day single; $2.00 per day double; and $1.33 per day triple.

**Dutch Inn, Royal Inn, Howard Johnson's and Travelodge. Selection to be made at time of booking.

"Orlando & Disney World"
$48⁵⁰ to $77⁰⁰•
4 DAYS/3 NIGHTS

- Eastern Airlines Exclusive: Two 9-ride Ticket Books for Walt Disney World, including admission to Disney World for two days.
- Roundtrip transfers between airport, hotel and Disney World OR
Compact for three 24 hour periods with unlimited mileage at additional cost as noted.* (Gas and Collision Damage Waiver not included.)

PER PERSON RATES Effective: through Dec. 15, 1975. European Plan

Hotel/Period	Double	Extra Night	Triple	Extra Night	Single	Extra Night
FLORIDA CENTER HOTELS						
1776 Inn	$50.88	$8.88	$41.92	$5.92	$77.76	$17.76
Rodeway Inn	51.50	9.00	44.67	6.67	72.50	16.00
Red Carpet Inn Int'l.	48.50	8.00	42.50	6.00	66.50	14.00
Gateway Inn	54.50	10.00	48.50	8.00	78.50	18.00
Travelodge Jetport	57.50	11.00	49.33	8.33	78.50	18.00
Howard Johnson Kirkman	60.50	12.00	48.50	8.00	84.50	20.00
Sheraton Olympic Villas	60.50	12.00	48.50	8.00	96.50	24.00
Quality Inn Int'l.	54.50	10.00	46.33	7.33	78.50	18.00
Hilton Inn South	65.00	13.50	55.33	10.33	81.50	19.00
Travelodge Int'l.	60.50	12.00	51.50	9.00	87.50	21.00
KISSIMMEE						
Hilton Inn Gateway	65.00	13.50	55.33	10.33	81.50	19.00
Howard Johnson Main Gate	63.50	13.00	54.50	10.00	90.50	22.00
Sheraton Lakeside	66.50	14.00	56.64	10.64	108.50	28.00
Hyatt of Orlando	75.50	17.00	58.33	11.33	126.50	34.00
Holiday Inn	55.00	9.50	49.67	7.67	79.00	17.00
World Inn	66.50	14.00	52.33	9.33	90.50	22.00
LAKE BUENA VISTA						
Motor Inn Plaza Hotels**						
through 12/19	77.00	17.50	63.50	13.00	129.50	35.00

IT5EA1GOCX

•Per person, double occupancy, air fare additional.

© Walt Disney Productions

"Tennis on the Gulf" Florida Gulf Coast
$38⁰⁵ to $55⁰⁰•
4 DAYS/3 NIGHTS

- Roundtrip transfers between Tampa airport and hotel or Sarasota airport and Colony Beach Resort.**
- Complimentary tennis.
- Complimentary chaise lounges and parking.
- Optional day at Walt Disney World available.

PER PERSON RATES Effective: through Dec. 15, 1975. **European Plan**

Hotel/Period	Double	Extra Night	Triple	Extra Night	Quad	Extra Night	Single	Extra Night
Belleview Gulf Beach & Tennis Club through 12/15	$44.80	$11.00	$36.85	$8.35	$32.80	$7.00	$71.80	$20.00
			4 Tennis Courts/No charge for children under 12.					
Don Cesar Resort Hotel through 12/15	50.80	13.00	41.80	10.00	37.30	8.50	77.80	22.00
			2 Tennis Courts/No charge for children under 14.					
Sheraton BelAir 9/9-12/11	38.05	8.75	32.35	6.85	29.50	5.90	55.30	14.50
			5 Tennis Courts/No charge for children under 18.					
Sheraton Sand-Key Hotel through 12/14	49.30	12.50	40.90	9.70	36.55	8.25	86.80	25.00
			2 Tennis Courts/No charge for children under 17.					
Colony Beach Resort/ Sarasota through 12/1	55.00	15.00*	75.10	21.70†	58.75	16.25†	100.00	30.00*
			2 Tennis Courts					

IT5EA1TMPWC8

• **Per person, double occupancy, air fare additional.**

*Rate is for one-bedroom apartment.
†Rate is for two-bedroom apartment.

**Optional Olin's sub-compact car with unlimited mileage available at $12 per day, $70 per week; in Sarasota, Budget available at $14.95 per day, $89.95 per week. Gas, oil and Collision Damage Waiver not included.

If optional car is desired, deduct $11.80 for transfers, and add car rate. Car may be picked up and dropped in Orlando, Tampa, Miami or Ft. Lauderdale at no extra cost. For Sarasota transfers, deduct $10.00.

"Destination Daytona Beach"
$24⁰⁰ to $40⁵⁰•
4 DAYS/3 NIGHTS

- Roundtrip airport transfers.*
- Optional day at Walt Disney World.**
- Cocktail at Daytona Beach nightspot.

PER PERSON RATES Effective: through Dec. 15, 1975. **European Plan**

Hotel/Period	Double	Extra Night	Triple	Extra Night	Quad	Extra Night	Single	Extra Night
Ramada Inn South 9/9-12/15	$24.00	$6.00	$21.00	$5.00	$19.50	$4.50	$42.00	$12.00
			No charge for children under 18.					
Thunderbird 8/26-12/15	28.50	7.50	24.00	6.00	21.75	5.25	48.00	14.00
			No charge for children under 18.					
Holiday Inns Beachside, Oceanside, & Surfside 9/1-12/15	28.50	7.50	27.00	7.00	24.00	6.00	48.00	14.00
			No charge for children under 18.					
Treasure Island Inn/Sheraton Inn 8/26-12/15	33.00	9.00	27.00	7.00	24.00	6.00	57.00	17.00
			No charge for children under 18.					
Quality Inn Oceanside 9/3-12/15	39.00	11.00	31.05	8.35	27.00	7.00	60.00	18.00
			No charge for children under 16.					
Daytona Hilton 9/8-12/15	40.50	11.50	34.05	9.35	30.75	8.25	62.00	19.00
			No charge for children under 18.					

IT5EA1TMPD3

• **Per person, double occupancy, air fare additional.**

*Optional Budget sub-compact available with unlimited mileage at $15 per day.
**Walt Disney World Option—Admission and transfer to WDW with 8 attractions—Adult: $16.50/Jr. (10-17): $16.00/Child (3-11): $10.85.

This folder contains only a few of Eastern's many vacation offerings. For more information consult your Travel Agent or Eastern.

Unless otherwise specified, meals, taxes, hotel service charges not included. Air fare and applicable security charges additional.

d. What is the difference in the rental cost of an Olin subcompact car and a

Budget car for one day? _____

e. Which place would you rather visit? _____

_____

Why?_____

_____

_____

5. FINDING AND INTERPRETING DETAILS IN TRAVEL BROCHURES
Use the information contained in the **Lion Country Safari** brochure on page 115 to answer the following:

a. In the section entitled "The Preserve,"

(1) You must stay in your car when you drive through this area. How are

you guided through?_____

(2) What word describes

(a) a group of ostriches?_____

(b) a group of lions?_____

(3) What two safety measures should you take when driving through?

(a) _____

(b) _____

(4) The brochure says you can get "eyeball-to-kneecap" with a giraffe.

Why did they use that phrase?_____

_____

_____

(5) What two types of "cats" can you see in the preserve?

(a) _____

(b) _____

From *Reading for Survival in Today's Society, Volume One*, ©1978 Goodyear Publishing Company, Inc.

Welcome to Lion Country! Check your camera and film supply, turn on our tour guide tape player and prepare to begin a safari through the most unusual jungle in the world.

Mother Nature, with a little help from friends, has placed all of our animals in a setting of lush green flora specifically designed for picture taking or viewing.

The first animal you'll no doubt encounter will be the ostrich. A colorful flock may be found manning the entrance to our jungle.

Check to make sure all windows are up and your motorcar doors are locked.

And don't forget our great cats — as if they would let you. Prides of majestic lions prowl a large portion of our jungle while just to the north an unusual family of shy and elusive cheetah move barely discernible through a maze of greenery.

Where but our jungle can one get "eyeball-to-kneecap" with a lofty giraffe, or "eyeball-to-horn" with a preponderate rhinoceros — all wandering free just the other side of your car window.

the PRESERVE

the VILLAGE

The Native Village Amusement Center separates our jungle from any other. Avian displays so colorful they shame a rainbow guide you through a New World of animal petting areas, art & craft shops and baby animals.

Walk past a multi-windowed maternity ward of exotic animals born right here in our jungle.

Or steer our zebra-striped miniature jeeps through a water-falled world of pink elephants, polka-dotted giraffe and close-enough-to-touch live animal displays.

And for those who like exercise, there's a fleet of outlandishly painted hippo-pedal boats set on sparkling Lake Shanalee.

The mile-long Kenya Express train ride takes you to the other end of the Dark Continent where you'll find a zany bird show, the Zambezi River ride and a host of animals you didn't see in the drive-through jungle.

Because our animals are wild, you might want to take another safari through the jungle after touring the Native Village — go through as many times as you'd like on the same day at no additional charge. Lion Country — it's a most unusual jungle.

b. In the section entitled "The Village,"

    (1) There are three types of transportation mentioned (not including walking). What are they?

        (a) _____

        (b) _____

        (c) _____

    (2) If you toured the jungle in the morning and you wanted to go back through it in the afternoon, would you have to pay again?_____

    (3) What compound word is used to mean "very near?" _____

        _____

    (4) The description of the Avian displays says they are "so colorful they shame a rainbow." Are the displays more or less colorful than a rainbow? _____

other ideas

    A. Call some hotels or motels in your town and request rates for a single and a double room. Compare the prices. If possible, discuss features some hotels/motels have that might be reasons for higher or lower charges.

    B. Create a travel poster, brochure, or small advertisement for one city in this country.

    C. Write literature describing the ideal city.

    D. Invite a travel agent to visit the class to discuss the purposes and advantages of engaging a travel agent to help plan a trip.

    E. Select a site to visit. One group plans the trip through a travel agent. Another group plans the same trip without the service of an agent. Transportation, lodging, cost of trip, clothing, sites of interest, etc. should be detailed. Compare the planning process and the price.

From *Reading for Survival in Today's Society,* Volume One, ©1978 Goodyear Publishing Company, Inc.

F. Travel agencies, national recreation bureaus, and embassies of foreign countries all dispense a variety of travel information. Write some of these types of agencies and request information concerning one particular foreign country. Use the materials received to design a travel display. Other items that might be included are:

- books concerning the geography, history, customs, and literature of the country;
- recordings of the country's folk music;
- "realia" from the country, such as a sombrero from Mexico or a pair of wooden shoes from Holland.

G. Use magazines containing advertisements of different places to visit. Analyze the advertisements according to items such as (1) the place farthest from your home; (2) the place nearest to your home; (3) the place to which you would have to take clothing other than what you wear at home; and (4) the place you would need a passport to visit.

key words & phrases

destination	vacation	cottage	complimentary
expenses	luxurious	climate	rustic
hospitality	villa	recreation	accommodations
dining	facilities	sightseer	continental
escort	entertain	chalet	reservation

self-evaluation

	date completed	possible score	your score	EXPERT	AVERAGE	FAIR	HELP!
1. Identifying special features in a vacation description		6					
2. Distinguishing between fact and opinion in travel literature		6					
3. Comparing hotel costs in one geographical area		7					
4. Comparing hotel costs in two different cities		7					
5. Finding and interpreting details in travel brochures		14					

CIRCLE **other ideas**
COMPLETED: A B C D E
       F G

TOTAL POSSIBLE POINTS: **40**

YOUR TOTAL POINTS:

How did you rate yourself?

name & date

dictionary

12

12

DICTIONARY

Few persons consult a dictionary on a daily basis; however, when they need to determine the correct spelling of a word, whether the word carries the meaning needed, or how the word is pronounced, a dictionary is the best source of information. Asking a friend may elicit a reply similar to "I'm not sure. Look it up in the dictionary." Students should be taught to relate the use of the dictionary to such life situations as correct spelling on job applications and selection of words for job-related duties.

Specific reading skills emphasized in this module are: (1) associating pronunciation key symbols with one's name; (2) relating pronunciation key symbols to critical words; (3) comparing dictionary definitions of the same word with meanings related to different occupations; (4) locating compound word and phrase definitions; and (5) using dictionary guide words.

materials

In addition to the dictionary illustrations in this module, make available for use in the classroom dictionaries of different types and sizes, including large, multivolume ones and thin, paperback ones. Include dictionaries on specific topics, such as space or medical terms.

survival reading skills

1. ASSOCIATING PRONUNCIATION KEY SYMBOLS WITH ONE'S NAME
Pronounce the parts of your name. Use the **Pronunciation Key** to locate key words that have each sound in your name. Write your name using pronunciation key symbols as if it were in the dictionary.

a. first name _____

b. middle name _____

c. last name _____

2. RELATING PRONUNCIATION KEY SYMBOLS TO CRITICAL WORDS
Beside each of the following important words, code the word sounds by using pronunciation key symbols. Then check the dictionary to determine how closely you keyed the words to the way the dictionary has them keyed.

a. emergency_____

b. antidote_____

c. exit_____

d. notice _____

3. COMPARING DICTIONARY DEFINITIONS OF THE SAME WORD WITH MEANINGS RELATED TO DIFFERENT OCCUPATIONS.
Below is a list of different occupations. Read the dictionary definitions for *bang* on page 123. On the line beside each occupation, write the definition a person writing or talking about that occupation might use.

a. Beautician _____

_____

_____

b. Carpenter using a hammer_____

_____

_____

c. Explosives expert _____

_____

_____

d. Cartoon artist_____

_____

_____

PRONUNCIATION KEY

The symbol ('), as in moth·er (muth'ər), blue' dev'ils, is used to mark primary stress; the syllable preceding it is pronounced with greater prominence than the other syllables in the word or phrase. The symbol ('), as in grand·moth·er (grand'muth'ər), buzz' bomb', is used to mark secondary stress; a syllable marked for secondary stress is pronounced with less prominence than one marked (') but with more prominence than those bearing no stress mark at all.

a	act, bat, marry	**i**	if, big, mirror, furniture	**p**	pot, supper, stop		indicate the sound of
ā	aid, cape, way	**ī**	ice, bite, pirate, deny	**r**	read, hurry, near		a *in* alone
â(r)	air, dare, Mary						e *in* system
ä	alms, art, calm			**s**	see, passing, miss		i *in* easily
				sh	shoe, fashion, push		o *in* gallop
b	back, cabin, cab	**j**	just, badger, fudge				u *in* circus
				t	ten, butter, bit		
ch	chief, butcher, beach	**k**	kept, token, make	**th**	thin, ether, path		occurs in unaccented syllables before l
				th	that, either, smooth		preceded by t, d, or
d	do, rudder, bed	**l**	low, mellow, all	**u**	up, love		n, or before n preceded by t or d to
				û(r)	urge, burn, cur		show syllabic quality, as in
e	ebb, set, merry	**m**	my, simmer, him	**v**	voice, river, live		cra·dle (krād'ᵊl)
e	equal, seat, bee, mighty						red·den (red'ᵊn)
		n	now, sinner, on	**w**	west, away		met·al (met'ᵊl)
ēr	ear, mere	**ng**	sing, Washington				men·tal (men't'ᵊl)
				y	yes, lawyer		and in accented syllables between ī and
f	fit, differ, puff	**o**	ox, box, wasp				r to show diphthongal quality, as in
		ō	over, boat, no	**z**	zeal, lazy, those		fire (fīᵊr) hire (hīᵊr)
g	give, trigger, beg	**ô**	ought, ball, raw	**zh**	vision, mirage		
		oi	oil, joint, joy				
		ōō	book, poor	**ə**	occurs only in unaccented syllables and		
h	hit, behave, hear	**ōō**	ooze, fool, too				
hw	white, nowhere	**ou**	out, loud, prow				

---

4. LOCATING COMPOUND WORD AND PHRASE DEFINITIONS

In the example on page 123, the word *bank* is part of each entry. Locate and write the appropriate *bank* word for each of the following:

a. A profession_____

b. A politician_____

c. What hasn't been spent in a bank account _____

d. A day during the week when the bank is closed _____

From *Reading for Survival in Today's Society*, Volume One, ©1978 Goodyear Publishing Company, Inc.

bang¹ (bang), *n.* **1.** a loud, sudden, explosive noise, as the discharge of a gun. **2.** a resounding stroke or blow: *an awful bang on the head.* **3.** *Informal.* a sudden movement or show of energy. **4.** *U.S. Slang.* sudden or intense pleasure; thrill or excitement: *to get a big bang out of movies.* —*v.t.* **5.** to strike or beat resoundingly; slam. —*v.i.* **6.** to strike violently or noisily. **7.** to make a loud, sudden, explosive noise. —*adv.* **8.** suddenly and loudly; abruptly or violently: *He fell bang against the wall.* **9.** directly; precisely; right: *He stood bang in the center of the flower bed.* [cf. Icel *banga* to beat, hammer, LG *bangen* to strike, beat]

bang² (bang), *n.* **1.** Usually, **bangs.** a fringe of hair combed or brushed forward over the forehead. —*v.t.* **2.** to cut (the hair) so as to form a fringe over the forehead. [short for BANGTAIL]

bang³ (bang), *n.* bhang.

e. Money borrowed from a bank _____

f. An evening when prizes are given away at a movie _____

g. A person who works in a bank _____

5. USING DICTIONARY GUIDE WORDS

Read the dictionary information on page 124. Using the guide words *bandleader* and *bank night*, locate the words described in the first two columns below. In the third column, write the guide word that appears at the top of the dictionary column in which you found your answer.

FIRST FOUR LETTERS IN WORD	HINT TO MEANING	GUIDE WORD
bane	has poisonous berries	_____
banj	a member of the guitar family	_____
bani	at the edge of a staircase	_____
band	an endless saw	_____
band	tennis practice	_____

Ban·ka (bang′kə), *n.* Bangka.

bank·a·ble (bang′kə bəl), *adj.* capable of being received, processed, or acted upon by a bank. [BANK² + -ABLE]

bank′ accept′ance, a draft endorsed or otherwise formally acknowledged by a bank on which it is drawn. Also called **banker's acceptance.**

bank′ account′, **1.** an account with a bank. **2.** balance standing to the credit of a depositor at a bank. Also called, *Brit.,* **banking account.**

bank′ annu′ity, Usually, **bank annuities.** consol.

bank′ bal′ance, **1.** balance standing to the credit of a depositor at a bank. **2.** *Finance.* the balance that a bank has in the clearing house at a given time.

bank′ bill′, a draft drawn by one bank on another, payable on demand or at a specified future date. Also called **banker's bill.**

bank·book (bangk′book′), *n.* a book held by a depositor in which a bank enters a record of his account. [BANK² + BOOK]

bank′ check′, **1.** a check that the depositor of a checking account draws on a bank for payment. **2.** See **cashier's check.**

bank′ clerk′, *Brit.* teller (def. 2).

bank′ depos′it, money placed in a bank against which the depositor can withdraw under prescribed conditions.

bank′ dis′count, interest on a loan, deducted in advance from the face value of the note.

bank′ draft′, a draft drawn by one bank on another.

bank·er¹ (bang′kər), *n.* **1.** a person employed by a bank, esp. as an executive or other official. **2.** *Games.* the keeper or holder of the bank. [BANK² + -ER²]

bank·er² (bang′kər), *n.* **1.** a vessel employed in the cod fishery on the banks off Newfoundland. **2.** a fisherman on such a vessel. **3.** *Australian.* a river near flood level, the water being almost bank high. [BANK¹ + -ER¹]

bank·er³ (bang′kər), *n.* a bench or table used by masons for dressing stones or bricks. [BANK³ + -ER¹]

bank′er's accep′tance. See **bank acceptance.**

bank′er's bill′. See **bank bill.**

Bank·head (bangk′hed), *n.* **1.** Tal·lu·lah (Brockman) (tə loō′lə brok′mən), born 1903, U.S. actress (daughter of William Brockman Bankhead). **2.** William Brockman, 1874–1940, U.S. politician, Speaker of the House 1936–40.

bank′ hol′iday, **1.** a weekday on which banks are closed by law; legal holiday. **2.** *Brit.* a secular day on which banks are closed, obligations then falling due being performable on the secular day next following.

bank·ing (bang′king), *n.* **1.** the business carried on by a bank or a banker. **2.** banking as a profession. [BANK² + -ING¹]

bank′ing account′, *Brit.* See **bank account.**

bank′ loan′, an amount of money loaned at interest by a bank to a borrower, usually on collateral security, for a certain period of time.

bank′ night′, *U.S. Informal.* an evening when prizes are awarded to members of the audience at a motion-picture theater.

bandleader 106 **bank night**

band·lead·er (band′lē′dər), *n.* the leader of a band.
band·mas·ter (band′mas′tər, -mä′stər), *n.* the conductor of a military band, circus band, etc.
Ban·doeng (bän′dŏong), *n.* Dutch name of **Bandung.**
ban·do·leer (ban′də·lēr′), *n.* a broad belt worn over the shoulder by soldiers and having a number of small loops or pockets, for containing a cartridge or cartridges. Also, **ban′do·lier′.** [earlier *bandollier* < MF *bando·liere,* fem. of *bandoullier* < Catalan *bandoler* member of a band of men (*bandol* (< Sp *bando* band¹) + -*er* -ier²)]
ban·do·line (ban′də·lēn′, -d′līn), *n.* a mucilaginous preparation made from quince seeds and used for smoothing, glossing, or waving the hair. [< F *bandeau* BANDEAU + L *linere*) (to) anoint, smear]
ban·dore (ban·dōr′, -dôr′, ban′dōr, -dôr), *n.* any of various obsolete musical instruments resembling the lute or the guitar. Also called **ban·do·ra** (ban·dōr′ə, -dôr′ə), **pandora, pandore.** [earlier *bandurion* < Sp *bandurria* < L *pandura* < Gk *pandoura* three-stringed musical instrument]
band′ saw′, *Mach.* a saw consisting of an endless toothed steel band passing over two wheels.
bands·man (bandz′mən), *n., pl.* **-men.** a musician who plays in a band.
band′ spec′trum, *Physics.* a spectrum consisting of groups of closely spaced lines, usually associated with excited molecules.
band·stand (band′stand′), *n.* a raised platform where the members of a band or orchestra sit while performing.
Ban·dung (bän′dŏong), *n.* a city in W Java, in Indonesia. 966,350 with suburbs, 1,028,215 (1961). Dutch, **Bandoeng.**
band·wag·on (band′wag′ən), *n.* **1.** a wagon, usually large and ornately decorated, for carrying a musical band, as in a circus parade, at the head of a procession. **2. be or jump on or aboard the bandwagon,** *U.S. Informal.* to support a candidate, cause, movement, etc., that seems assured of success.
band·width (band′width′, -with′), *Radio.* a certain range of frequencies within a band.
ban·dy (ban′dē), *v.,* **-died, -dy·ing,** *adj., n., pl.* **-dies.** —*v.t.* **1.** to throw or strike to and fro or from side to side, as a ball in tennis. **2.** to pass from one to another or back and forth; give and take; trade; exchange: *to bandy blows; to bandy words.* —*adj.* **3.** (of legs) having a bend or crook outward; bowed. —*n.* **4.** an early form of tennis. [? < Sp *bandear*) (to) conduct, bandy, orig. help, i.e. serve as member of a band of men]
ban·dy-leg·ged (ban′dē·leg′id, -legd′), *adj.* having crooked legs; bowlegged.
bane (bān), *n.* **1.** a person or thing that ruins or spoils: *Gambling was the bane of his existence.* **2.** a deadly poison (often used in combination, as in the names of poisonous plants): *wolfsbane; henbane.* **3.** death, destruction, or ruin. **4.** *Literary.* a thing that causes death or destroys life. [ME; OE *bana* slayer; c. Icel *bani* death, murderer, OHG *bano* death; akin to Goth *banja* wound, Gk *phonos* slaughter]
bane·ber·ry (bān′ber′ē, -bər·ē), *n., pl.* **-ries. 1.** any ranunculaceous plant of the genus *Actaea,* bearing poisonous red or white berries. **2.** the berry of such a plant.
bane·ful (bān′fəl), *adj.* destructive, pernicious, or poisonous: *baneful herbs.* —**bane′ful·ly,** *adv.* —**bane′ful·ness,** *n.* —Syn. deadly, harmful, noxious; venomous.
Banff (bamf), *n.* a resort town in a national reserve (**Banff National Park**), 2,585 sq mi) in the Rocky Mountains in SW Alberta, Canada. 3,418 (1961).

+ -iss- -tion²] —**ban′ish·er,** *n.* —**ban′ish·ment,** *n.* —Syn. 1. exile, expatriate, outlaw; deport.
ban·is·ter (ban′i·stər), *n.* **1.** a baluster, esp. a one at the edge of a staircase. **2.** Sometimes **banisters,** the balustrade of a staircase. Also, **bannister.** [var. of BALUSTER]
Ban·jer·ma·sin (bän′jər·mä′sin), *n.* a seaport on the S coast of Borneo, in Indonesia. 212,683 (est. 1961). Also, **Bandjermasin.**

ban·jo (ban′jō), *n., pl.* **-jos, -joes.** a musical instrument of the guitar family, having a circular body covered in front with tightly stretched parchment and either four or five strings played with the fingers or a plectrum. [var. of BANDORE] —**ban′jo·ist,** *n.*

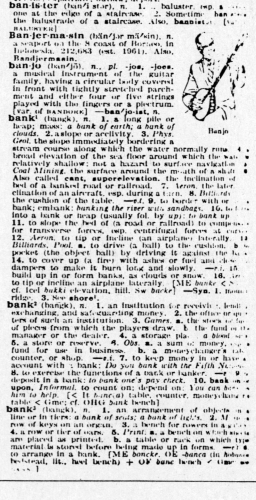

Banjo

bank¹ (bangk), *n.* **1.** a long pile or heap; mass: *a bank of earth; a bank of clouds.* **2.** a slope or acclivity. **3.** *Phys. Geol.* the slope immediately bordering a stream course along which the water normally runs. **4.** a broad elevation of the sea floor around which the water is relatively shallow; not a hazard to surface navigation. **5.** *Coal Mining.* the surface around the mouth of a shaft. **6.** Also called **cant, superelevation.** the inclination of the bed of a banked road or railroad. **7.** *Aeron.* the later inclination of an aircraft, esp. during a turn. **8.** *Billiards.* the cushion of the table. —*v.t.* **9.** to border with or bank; embank: *banking the river with sandbags.* **10.** to form into a bank or heap (usually fol. by *up*): *to bank up.* **11.** to slope the bed of (a road or railroad) to compensate for transverse forces, esp. centrifugal forces at curves. **12.** *Aeron.* to tip or incline (an airplane) laterally. **13.** *Billiards, Pool.* **a.** to drive (a ball) to the cushion. **b.** to pocket (the object ball) by driving it against the bank. **14.** to cover up (a fire) with ashes or fuel and close dampers to make it burn long and slowly. —*v.i.* **15.** build up in or form banks, as clouds or snow. **16.** *Aeron.* to tip or incline an airplane laterally. [ME *banke* < S. cf. Icel *bakki* elevation, hill, Sw *backe*] —Syn. 1. mound, ridge. 3. See **shore¹.**
bank² (bangk), *n.* **1.** an institution for receiving, lending, exchanging, and safeguarding money. **2.** the office or quarters of such an institution. **3.** *Games.* **a.** the stock or fund of pieces from which the players draw. **b.** the fund of the manager or the dealer. **4.** a storage place. **a blood bank. 5.** a store or reserve. **6.** *Obs.* **a.** a sum of money, esp. a fund for use in business. **b.** a moneychanger's table, counter, or shop. —*v.i.* **7.** to keep money in or have an account with a bank: *Do you bank with the Fifth National?* **8.** to exercise the functions of a bank or banker. —*v.t.* **9.** deposit in a bank: *to bank one's pay check.* **10. bank on or upon,** *Informal.* to count on; depend on: *You can bank on him to help.* [< It *banca*(a) table, counter, moneychanger's table < Gmc; cf. OHG *bank* bench]
bank³ (bangk), *n.* **1.** an arrangement of objects in a line or in tiers: *a bank of seats; a bank of lights.* **2.** Mus. a row of keys on an organ. **3.** a bench for rowers in a galley. **4.** a row or tier of oars. **5.** *Print.* **a.** a bench on which slugs are placed as printed. **b.** a table or rack on which type material is stored before being made up in forms. —*v.t.* **6.** to arrange in a bank. [ME *boncke*, OE *-banca* (in *hobanca* bedstead, lit., heel bench) + OF *banc* bench < Gmc; see BANK²]

other ideas

A. Select at least five specialized words associated with one profession. Locate these words in a dictionary and notice other definitions of them.

B. Identify three words associated with one of your hobbies. Write definitions of the words. Compare your definition with those in a dictionary.

C. Write a letter as if you were applying for a certain job. When the letter is finished, circle each word that is related to the job. Using a dictionary, check to see if you spelled these words correctly.

D. Hold a class relay race. Divide the class into five or six teams. Each team must have a dictionary, a piece of chalk, and access to space on the chalkboard. Call a word. The first person in each team finds the word in the dictionary, goes to the chalkboard and writes the guide words at the top of the page on which the word was found. *Variations:* Write the phonetic spelling; write the number of the definition that best fits the way the word is used in a sentence.

E. Play Dictionary Bingo. Prepare a set of cards with phonetic spellings in each box. The teacher or another student calls out a word. Cover the phonetic spelling of the word. *Variation:* Put entry words on the Bingo card and call out dictionary guide words.

key words & phrases

prefix	homonym	denotation	compound
suffix	synonym	connotation	illustration
affix	syllables	etymology	abridged
entry	variant	alphabetical	definition
rhyme	derivation	diacritical	pronunciation

self-evaluation

	date completed	possible score	your score	EXPERT	AVERAGE	FAIR	HELP!
1. Associating pronunciation key symbols with one's name		3					
2. Relating pronunciation key symbols to critical words		4					
3. Comparing dictionary definitions of the same word with meanings related to different occupations		4					
4. Locating compound word and phrase definitions		7					
5. Using dictionary guide words		5					

CIRCLE **other ideas**
COMPLETED: A B C D E

TOTAL POSSIBLE POINTS: **23**

YOUR TOTAL POINTS:

How did you rate yourself?

name & date

telephone directory

13

13

TELEPHONE DIRECTORY

The telephone is one of the most powerful instruments of communication in today's society. Whether on home telephones, at pay stations, or from businesses, Americans make more than 600 million telephone calls a day.[1] *In 1974, 94 percent of all households in the United States had a telephone.*[2] In almost all of these homes, there was at least one telephone directory.

It is extremely important for persons of all ages to know how to read the telephone directory accurately. Some telephone companies charge for calls to the information operator requesting local telephone numbers. The outcome of an emergency may be determined by how quickly someone at the scene can locate and dial appropriate telephone numbers and clearly explain the type of help that is needed and where.

Specific reading lessons emphasized in this module are: (1) learning to locate emergency numbers; (2) noting long distance area codes; (3) locating information in the yellow pages; (4) reading information about telephone services; and (5) finding information in the white pages.

materials

Make available in the classroom copies of local telephone directories. Out-of-date copies are fine for these lessons. Suggest students bring telephone books from home, and contact the telephone company for free literature.

[1]United States Bureau of the Census, *Statistical Abstract of the United States: 1975* (96th ed.; Washington, D.C.: U.S. Bureau of the Census, 1975), p. 515.
[2]Ibid.

survival reading skills

1. LEARNING TO LOCATE EMERGENCY NUMBERS

Read the **emergency numbers** information on page 130.

a. Write the telephone numbers you would call for each of the following:

(1) An ambulance _____

(2) The FBI _____

(3) A fire in Creedmoor_____

(4) The state highway patrol _____

(5) The Poison Control Center_____

(6) The police_____

(7) The U.S. Secret Service _____

(8) The Information and Referral Center _____

b. If you cannot stay at the telephone, what information should you give the

operator when reporting an emergency?_____

_____

_____

c. What telephone numbers are you supposed to write on this page?_____

_____

_____

_____

d. Using a local telephone book, locate the page where emergency numbers and other information are found, and learn the emergency numbers.

2. NOTING LONG DISTANCE AREA CODES

Refer to a local telephone directory and write the area code for each of the following places:

a. Bakersfield, California   _____

b. Richmond, Virginia   _____

From *Reading for Survival in Today's Society*, Volume One, ©1978 Goodyear Publishing Company, Inc.

emergency numbers

Write in the telephone numbers you will need in case of emergency. Obtain your "police" and "fire" numbers from the list on this page.

	Durham	Creedmoor	Butner	Stem
fire	911 emergency only	911	911	528-0312
police	911 emergency only	911	911	911

Emergency calls of any type may also be made from emergency telephone call boxes located in the vicinity of most traffic signal lights, schools, hospitals and other strategic locations.

state highway patrol — emergency only ——————————————— 911

doctor — office ———————————————
home ———————————————

ambulance ——————————————— 911

Information & Referral Center ——————————————— 683-2521
Contact Teleministry ——————————————— 683-1595
Crisis & Suicide Center ——————————————— 688-5504
Poison Control Center ——————————————— 684-8111

FBI — If No Answer Call Charlotte (Toll Chg.) — 682-5617 / 372-5485

US Secret Service — Charlotte, N. C. (Toll Chg.) ——————————————— 372-0711

or dial "OPERATOR" in any emergency and say for example
"I want to report a fire at—"
or "I want a policeman at—."
If you cannot stay at the telephone, tell the "OPERATOR" the exact location where help is needed.

From "Reading for Survival in Today's Society, Volume One," ©1978 Goodyear Publishing Company, Inc.

   c. Jacksonville, Florida   _____

   d. Hershey, Pennsylvania   _____

   e. Kalamazoo, Michigan   _____

   f. Hawaii (all locations)   _____

   g. Galveston, Texas   _____

   h. Schenectady, New York   _____

   i. Akron, Ohio   _____

   j. Wyoming (all locations)   _____

   k. Kokomo, Indiana   _____

   l. Dodge City, Kansas   _____

   m. Rome, Georgia   _____

   n. Colorado (all locations)   _____

   o. Muskogee, Oklahoma   _____

3. LOCATING INFORMATION IN THE YELLOW PAGES

Read the listings and advertisements on page 132, and answer the following questions:

   a. What is the telephone number of the retirement home? _____

_____

   b. What is the address of the Waffle Inn? _____

   c. What is the telephone number of Elycroft Farm on River Road? _____

_____

   d. During what hours is the Village Tavern open? _____

_____

   e. What two features does the Le May's advertisement list?

      (1) _____

      (2) _____

Restaurants-(Cont'd)

University Restaurant
46 E Geer 174-6915
(See Ad This Classification)
VILLA DINNER THEATRE
1145 Hillview.....419-2308
Village Coffee Shop
Wood Rd 263-1089
Village Tavern
4867 Holloway.....419-1944
WAFFLE INN
1213 N Duke 419-1571

WESTERN BEEF HOUSE

Choice Western beef
Open Daily
11A.M. - 7 days a week
174-9857

Whesell's Drive Inn
Hwy. 52...........263-3814
White's Grill
784-5th...........174-9632

Retirement Communities
See Also Nursing Homes
Royal Retirement Homes Inc
5196 Watts Av......263-7056

Retirement Homes

FELLOWSHIP RETIREMENT HOME
PRIVATE
REASONABLE RATES
Rt. 6 419-2084

Reweavers

WEAVERS INC -------------

Burns Tears Holes
FAST SERVICE

234 Green 263-4765

Riding Academies

Elycroft Farm
River Rd 419-3701
ELYCROFT FARM _____
Everything in Horses
Jumping - Boarding
Hunt - Tack - Feed
2234 Green
River Rd 419-3701

From *Reading for Survival in Today's Society*, Volume One, ©1978 Goodyear Publishing Company, Inc.

f. Do you need to make reservations to eat at the Barn Steak House?

_____

g. Locate the name and telephone number of a restaurant on Hillview.

_____

h. What is the name of the restaurant that serves Indian and Italian food?

_____

4. READING INFORMATION ABOUT TELEPHONE SERVICES

Use a local telephone book and answer the following questions. If the answers are not in the directory and are not known by class members, ask a telephone company representative.

a. What is the charge for installing one desk telephone in a home? _____

_____

b. What is the basic cost per month to have one wall telephone and one

desk telephone in a home?_____

_____

c. If you make a call and it is answered by an automatic answering set, what

should you do? _____

_____

_____

d. If someone comes to your home and says he or she is from the telephone

company and you are not sure, what should you do?_____

_____

e. What is the cost of making a person-to-person weekday long distance

call for three minutes from your home to Hawaii or Alaska?_____

_____

f. What is the cost of making a person-to-person weekday long distance

call for three minutes from your home to Japan? _____

g. If you need to call overseas, what are the first two things you should tell the operator?

(1) _____

(2) _____

5. FINDING INFORMATION IN THE WHITE PAGES
Refer to the **white pages list** on page 135 and answer the following questions:

a. What is the occupation of William S. Browning?_____

b. What is Cathy Broyles's address?_____

c. Which Browning lives on Wilshire Court?_____

d. What is the telephone number of each of the following:

(1) City Hall_____

(2) City Manager's office _____

(3) Payroll–City Hall_____

(4) W. H. Bruce at Dixon Apartments_____

(5) Brownsville Chamber of Commerce_____

other ideas

A. Using the white pages in the telephone book, locate the telephone numbers of some of the students in your class.

B. Using the yellow pages, locate listings of stores selling the same type of items, and at least three stores where items of a markedly different nature are sold.

C. Make a shopping list of at least ten items. Exchange your list for one written by another student, and use the yellow pages to locate stores selling items on the list. The list should include a variety of items, such as:

1 pair boots	battery for a hearing aid
set of guitar strings	outdoor carpet
50 feet of ¼″ rope	book about travel in England
Kodak camera lens	Danish cheese
grass seed	paper tape for an adding machine

D. Make up a phone directory for the students in your class or school. Be sure to question each student about his or her yellow page listing. For example, students may wish to be listed under such headings as:

Babysitting Services	Lawn and Garden Work
Bicycle Repair	Tennis Lessons

Browning Susan 31 Wade Rd. 468-3217
Browning T A 3106 Craig St. 329-3574
Browning Thomas Wilshire Ct. 329-0954
Browning Virginia Mrs
    756 Clark St. 590-1456
Browning William B
    29 Hamilton Rd. 468-3928
Browning William S atty
    Ofc 14 Main St. 590-7164
    Res 58 Court Lane... 468-1637
Browning Willis 41-9th 590-4450
BROWNSVILLE CARPET CENTER
    3489 First St. 590-3531
    Or 590-3532
BROWNSVILLE CHAMBER OF COMMERCE
    605 Bank Bldg. 590-2134
BROWNSVILLE CITY GOVERNMENT
    Information for City Government
        City Hall 590-0505
    Administration Department of
        Director City Hall 590-1351
        Finance Director
            City Hall 590-1965
        Comptroller Division
            City Hall 590-1984
            Accounting City Hall 590-8643
            Payroll City Hall 590-8175
        Tax Office-Tax Collections And Assessments
            City Hall 590-4932
        Water and Sewer Customer Services City Hall
        Water Bills and Service City Hall 590-1612
    Building-Electrical-Plumbing and Heating Permits Inspection Division
        865 E Club 468-1919
    Cemetery Division
        Brownsville Cemetery
        Green Rd. 329-0143
        Oaklane Cemetery
        Rigsbee Ave. 468-3621
    City Manager
        City Hall 590-4560
    Election Board
        226 Holloway 468-1975
    Fire Department
        (Fire Calls Only) 118
        Routine Business 590-0101
    Garbage Collection 590-0024
    Libraries .... See Brown County
    Police Department
        Emergency Only 118
        For Other Calls 590-1112
    Transportation
        City Hall 590-1156
Broxton Carl 91 Drew Rd. 468-2938
Broyles Cathy Mrs.
    616 Granby 329-7698
Bruce W H Dixon Apts. 329-2440

E. Collect phone books from different cities. Compare the information included which does *not* relate to phones or the phone company (excluding the yellow pages). For example, directories may include maps of historical sites, calendars, and/or zip code maps.

key words & phrases

party	direct dial	emergency	residence
collect	extension	area code	telecommunication
directory	classified	mouthpiece	assistance
local	customer	receiver	person-to-person
dial	information	operator	station-to-station

self-evaluation

	date completed	possible score	your score	EXPERT	AVERAGE	FAIR	HELP!
1. Learning to locate emergency numbers		11					
2. Noting long distance area codes		15					
3. Locating information in the yellow pages		9					
4. Reading information about telephone services		8					
5. Finding information in the white pages		8					

CIRCLE **other ideas** COMPLETED: A B C D E

TOTAL POSSIBLE POINTS: 51

YOUR TOTAL POINTS:

How did you rate yourself?

name & date

From *Reading for Survival in Today's Society, Volume One.* © 1978 Goodyear Publishing Company, Inc.

job application forms

14

14

JOB APPLICATION FORMS

Jobs requiring no reading or writing skills are definitely an endangered species. White-collar jobs, which now constitute over half of the available jobs and are on the increase,[1] usually entail some form of paperwork. Many persons in so-called action jobs (for example, firemen and policemen) must fill out reports, and manual laborers frequently follow complicated printed plans or directions.

Ordinarily the first step in obtaining a job is applying for it. While some positions can be had for the asking, it is necessary to competently complete detailed application forms to be considered for others. Students should be introduced to the basic vocabulary and forms associated with obtaining employment.

Specific reading lessons emphasized in this module are: (1) associating words and pictures with different careers; (2) identifying specialized vocabulary on some job application forms; (3) completing mock job application forms; (4) correlating various career contributions with a given topic; and (5) recognizing job responsibilities with local businesses.

materials

Suggest students collect and bring to class a variety of forms and related information pertaining to different kinds of jobs.

[1] United States Bureau of the Census, *Statistical Abstract of the United States: 1975* (96th ed.; Washington, D.C.: U.S. Bureau of the Census, 1975), p. 359.

survival reading skills

1. ASSOCIATING WORDS AND PICTURES WITH DIFFERENT CAREERS

Select one career area, such as manufacturing, medicine, agriculture, or electronics. Using old magazines, cut out at least ten pictures associated with that career. Paste each picture on one side of a card, and on the back of the card write words describing how the picture relates to the career. Add any specialized words related to the career. Compare your cards and word lists with those of other students.

SAMPLE CAREER VOCABULARY

Beautician

hair	blow dry	tint	nail polish
comb	hair net	wash	lipstick
brush	permanent wave	set	shampoo
wig	scissors	fingernails	rinse
rollers	bleach	manicure	setting lotion

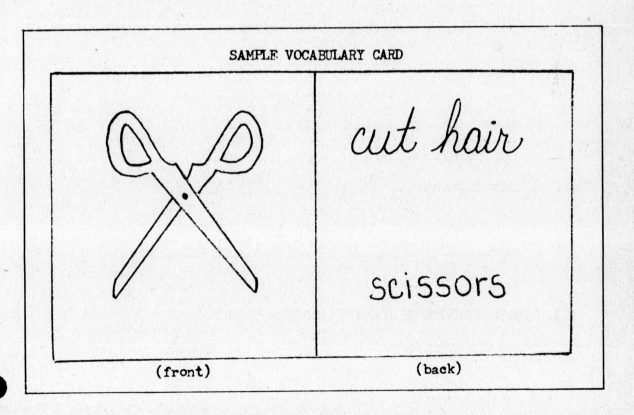

SAMPLE VOCABULARY CARD

(front)   (back)

From *Reading for Survival in Today's Society*, Volume One, ©1978 Goodyear Publishing Company, Inc.

2. IDENTIFYING SPECIALIZED VOCABULARY ON SOME JOB APPLICATION FORMS

Use a dictionary, if necessary, to identify the meaning of each of these terms as they would be used with reference to job application forms.

a. position _____

_____

b. citizen _____

_____

c. work experience _____

_____

d. recent _____

_____

e. references _____

_____

f. applicant _____

_____

g. signature _____

_____

h. health _____

_____

i. present employer _____

_____

j. salary _____

_____

3. COMPLETING MOCK JOB APPLICATION FORMS

Create an imaginary person applying for a job. Complete the six sections on the **job application form** (pages 141 and 142)[2] as if that person were seriously trying to get the job.

[2]Changes in laws may make it unlawful to include certain items on job application forms. Discuss such changes.

KERR DRUGS
APPLICATION FOR EMPLOYMENT

PERSONAL INFORMATION

Date _____

Name _____ Age _____ Sex _____

Permanent Address _____ City _____ State _____ Zip _____

Phone Number _____ Own Home _____ Rent _____ Board _____

Date of Birth _____ Social Security No. _____ US Citizen: Yes ___ No ___

Height _____ Weight _____ Color of Hair _____ Color of Eyes _____

Married _____ Single _____ Widowed _____ Divorced _____ Separated _____

Number of Children _____ Dependents Other Than Wife or Children _____

Relatives in Our Employ (state name & department) _____

Referred by _____

EMPLOYMENT DESIRED

Position _____ Date You Can Start _____ Salary Desired _____

Are You Employed Now? _____ If So May We Inquire of Your Present Employer? _____

Ever Applied to this Company Before? _____ Where? _____ When? _____

EDUCATION

	Name & Location	Years	Date Graduated	Subjects Studied
Grammar School	_____	_____	_____	_____
	_____			
High School	_____	_____	_____	_____
	_____			
College	_____	_____	_____	_____
	_____			
Trade, Business or Correspondence School	_____	_____	_____	_____
	_____			

Subjects of Special Study or Research Work _____

What Foreign Languages Do You Speak Fluently? Read _____ Write _____

From Reading for Survival in Today's Society, Volume One, ©1978 Goodyear Publishing Company, Inc.

US Military or Naval Service_____ Rank_____

Present Membership in National Guard or Reserves _____

Activities Other Than Religious (Civic, Fraternal, Athletic, etc.)_____

_____

FORMER EMPLOYERS: List last four employers, starting with last one first.

Date	Name and Address of Employer	Salary	Reason for Leaving
From _____	_____	_____	_____
To _____	_____		_____
From _____	_____	_____	_____
To _____	_____		_____
From _____	_____	_____	_____
To _____	_____		_____
From _____	_____	_____	_____
To _____	_____		_____

REFERENCES: Give below the names of three persons not related to you whom you have known at least one year.

NAME	ADDRESS	BUSINESS	HOW LONG
_____	_____	_____	_____
_____	_____	_____	_____
_____	_____	_____	_____

PHYSICAL RECORD

List any Defects_____

Were You Ever Injured?_____ Give Details _____

Have You Any Defects in Hearing?_____ Vision?_____ Speech?_____

In Case of Emergency Notify _____
                              (name)   (address)   (phone)

"I authorize investigation of all statements contained in this application. I understand that misrepresentation or omission of facts called for is cause for dismissal. Further, I understand and agree that my employment is for no definite period and may, regardless of the date of payment of my wages and salary, be terminated at any time without any previous notice."

Date_____ Signature _____

From Reading for Survival in Today's Society, Volume One; ©1978 Goodyear Publishing Company, Inc.

4. CORRELATING VARIOUS CAREER CONTRIBUTIONS WITH A GIVEN TOPIC

In the space below, paste a magazine picture that has many details. Draw lines from 20 items in the picture, and on each line write the name of one career you can associate with that part of the picture. For example, if there is a table in the picture, you might write lumberpersons, carpenters, furniture refinishers, painters, or caster manufacturers. Write the word(s) for only one career on the line, and be prepared to explain how you associated that career with the item.

5. RECOGNIZING JOB RESPONSIBILITIES WITH LOCAL BUSINESSES
Select at least four different business advertisements in the newspaper. For each, write the names of different career persons who work in that business. Discuss the kinds of jobs they perform.

other ideas

A. Conduct mock interviews for different kinds of jobs between a possible future employer and a person seeking employment. Stress qualifications, duties of the employee, and responsibilities of the employer.

B. Look in the newspaper classified advertisements at the section on jobs available. Underline in the job descriptions the qualifications needed. Discuss where and how these qualifications might be met.

C. Some occupations require extensive training. For example, becoming a doctor may mean attending school for more than twenty years! Determine the basic educational requirements for various professions, for example, doctor, lawyer, professor, or accountant, by looking in college catalogs and/or checking with licensing boards or bureaus.

D. Organize a Career Day in your school or class. Have each student come dressed as a person in a particular occupation and bring some props or hints. For example, although a student dressed as an electrician might wear ordinary overalls, he or she could also bring a light bulb, a socket, and some electrical tape or wiring. Reserve some time for each student to give a short description of his or her chosen occupation.

E. Within even the smallest community, there is a wealth of "people" resources. Why not set aside a portion of each month or week for a Career Information Session? Different persons from the community might be invited to each session to discuss such matters as:
- why they chose their particular field;
- what they like most, and least, about their job; and
- qualifications for their occupation.

On days when the class wishes to discuss a major occupation or profession, a panel of experts (for example, four lawyers) might be invited to give their views on these topics.

F. Discuss the personal and physical characteristics necessary for certain jobs. For example, it is taken for granted that teachers should have patience and construction workers should have strength, but should teachers necessarily be strong? Do construction workers need patience? And to what degree?

From *Reading for Survival in Today's Society, Volume One,* ©1978 Goodyear Publishing Company, Inc.

From *Reading for Survival in Today's Society*, Volume One, ®1978 Goodyear Publishing Company, Inc.

key words & phrases

birthdate	degree	practical	recommendation
title	marital	reference	qualifications
address	status	relative	attended
education	diploma	spouse	extracurricular
institution	duties	relevant	disability

self-evaluation

	date completed	possible score	your score	EXPERT	AVERAGE	FAIR	HELP!
1. Associating words and pictures with different careers		10					
2. Identifying specialized vocabulary on some job application forms		10					
3. Completing "mock" job application forms		6					
4. Correlating various career contributions with a given topic		20					
5. Recognizing job responsibilities with local businesses		4					

CIRCLE **other ideas**
COMPLETED: A B C D E
                      F

TOTAL POSSIBLE POINTS: **50**

YOUR TOTAL POINTS:

How did you rate yourself?

bank information

15

15

BANK INFORMATION

Most persons are convinced that it is not wise to keep their money hidden at home. They prefer the safety provided and the interest paid by a banking institution. For most of these persons, the bank serves as a place to deposit and withdraw monies from a checking account. For fewer persons, the bank also houses savings accounts and lends large sums of money for purchasing homes or automobiles. For still fewer persons, the bank acts as the trust agent for minor children and estates. *Directly or indirectly, banks affect the lives of every person in today's society*. All persons need to learn how to deposit and withdraw funds and how to keep records of these transactions.

Specific reading lessons emphasized in this module are: (1) finding the meaning of selected basic words associated with banking; (2) locating the meaning of more complicated banking terms; (3) learning important basic facts about writing checks; (4) noting items on savings withdrawal and savings deposit slips; and (5) completing a form to open a checking account.

materials

Students should collect and bring to class a variety of bank literature and forms. **Caution:** If actual checks are used, write *VOID* across each one.

survival reading skills

1. FINDING THE MEANING OF SELECTED BASIC WORDS ASSOCIATED WITH BANKING .

On the line following each word or phrase below, write the meaning that relates to banking. If necessary, refer to a dictionary, or look at the illustrations in this module and notice how the word or phrase is used.

a. check _____

_____

b. signature card _____

_____

c. deposit _____

_____

d. transaction _____

_____

e. savings account _____

_____

f. checking account _____

_____

g. currency _____

_____

h. average balance _____

_____

i. endorse _____

_____

j. sufficient funds _____

_____

From *Reading for Survival in Today's Society*, Volume One, ©1978 Goodyear Publishing Company, Inc.

DEFINITIONS OF BANKING TERMS

ACCOUNT NUMBER is a number identifying a checking, savings or loan account. On most personalized checks, it is the second set of figures imprinted in magnetic ink (⑈ 234⑈ 567 on your practice checks). This number is important to assure accurate processing of your checks. If not pre-imprinted on your check or deposit slip, the number should be written in by you.

BANK ROUTING SYMBOLS are numbers assigned to banks and used for the routing of checks to the right bank. They are located in two places on most checks—as the first eight numbers in magnetic ink characters along the bottom edge and as a fraction in the upper right corner.

BANK STATEMENT is a record of a customer's checking account prepared for him monthly. On the statement are listed all deposits made and all checks paid together with cost of service and balance information.

SERVICE CHARGES are made by the bank to cover costs incurred in processing checks. At many banks there is no service charge when a customer maintains a minimum deposit balance of $100.

COST OF SERVICE is a fee paid the bank for processing checks to an account. This fee is paid only when the cost of processing checks is greater than an allowance made for the amount on deposit.

FEDERAL DEPOSIT INSURANCE is provided on account balances up to $20,000. Participating banks have an FDIC membership sign at each teller window.

FEDERAL RESERVE SYSTEM is the central banking system in the United States operating primarily as a bank for banks. The system is composed of twelve district banks with branches. The Carolinas are in the 5th District and are served by the Federal Reserve Bank of Richmond with a branch in Charlotte.

MAGNETIC INK is used to print special figures (bank code, account number, and amount) along the bottom edge of modern personalized checks and deposit slips. Many banks have machines which can read the magnetic numbers, thus enabling computers to sort and post checks and deposits.

TRUST COMPANY manages money, investments and other property for others through settling estates, administering retirement and other trusts and serving as an agent in specialized business and investment activities.

From *Reading for Survival in Today's Society*, Volume One. © 1978 Goodyear Publishing Company, Inc.

2. LOCATING THE MEANING OF MORE COMPLICATED BANKING TERMS
Refer to the **Definitions of Banking Terms** on page 150 and answer the following questions:

a. What is the maximum account balance covered by Federal Deposit Insurance? _____

b. What is the account number used in the definition?_____

c. Which set of the numbers on a check is the account number and where is it found?

(1) _____

(2) _____

d. What kind of ink is used to print special information on personalized checks and deposit slips? _____

e. Where are the bank routing symbols found on a check? _____

_____

_____

f. At many banks, there is no service charge when a customer keeps a balance of $_____.

3. LEARNING IMPORTANT BASIC FACTS ABOUT WRITING CHECKS
Read the **Dos and Don'ts of Using Checks** on page 152 and write *do* or *don't* to answer each of the following:

a. Sign your name to an incomplete check _____

b. Write your check with ink_____

c. Write a check when you do not have an account in the bank _____

d. Make a check payable to cash before you go to a grocery store to cash it

_____

e. Have the figures (numbers) and written words for the numbers the same

_____

f. Write over the face of a check _____

DOs AND DON'Ts OF USING CHECKS

DO write your check with ink.

DO always sign your name to a check exactly as you signed the bank's signature card.

DO be sure the figures and the written amount are exactly the same.

DO deposit or cash promptly all checks payable to you.

DO consult your banker if you have a question about any transaction.

DO NOT sign your name to an incomplete check.

DO NOT write a check if you do not have sufficient funds in your account.

DO NOT write a check if you do not have an account established with the bank.

DO NOT alter, write over, or erase on the face of a check.

DO NOT endorse a check unless you want to guarantee it.

DO NOT make a check payable to cash unless it is to be cashed in the bank.

DO NOT endorse a check until you are ready to deposit or cash it.

4. **NOTING ITEMS ON SAVINGS WITHDRAWAL AND SAVINGS DEPOSIT SLIPS**

   Refer to the **savings withdrawal slip** on page 153 to answer the following questions:

   a. Where on the slip does a person write the account number? _____

   _____

   b. The amount is to be written in two ways. What are they?

   (1) _____

   (2) _____

   c. Where does the person sign his or her name? _____

   _____

From Reading for Survival in Today's Society, Volume One. ©1978 Goodyear Publishing Company, Inc.

From *Reading for Survival in Today's Society*, Volume One, ©1978 Goodyear Publishing Company, Inc.

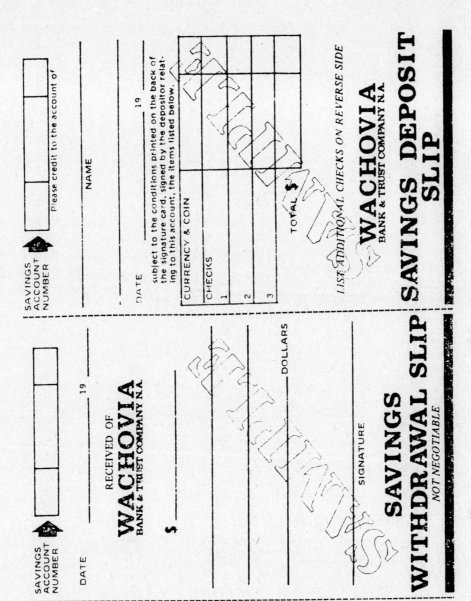

SAVINGS

Deposit accounts on which interest is paid and which are not subject to check are known as Savings Accounts.

How To Save

1. Make up your mind to save.

2. Have an objective – Christmas, hobby, vacation, education, automobile, rainy day, etc.

3. Save systematically. Small funds deposited regularly can quickly increase to a substantial amount. With Save-O-Matic the bank does this automatically for a checking customer, transferring a designated sum each month to his savings account.

Daily Interest is computed from the day of deposit to day of withdrawal at the rate of 5 percent per year. It is compounded daily and paid monthly.

Refer to the **savings deposit slip** on page 153 to answer the following questions:

d. Before a person writes any figures, what information should the person write on the slip?

(1) _____

(2) _____

(3) _____

e. Complete the sample savings deposit slip as if you deposited $18.76 in currency and coin, one check from Benbow, Inc., for $25.89, and one check from Atlantis Company for $89.67. Total the amount and write it in the appropriate place.

Refer to the paragraphs on page 153 to answer the following:

f. What tips does this bank give about how to save money?

(1) _____

(2) _____

(3) _____

g. Daily interest is computed at _____ percent each year.

---

1. Checking Account

Acct. No. _____

For Bank Use Only

Please have my Personal Banker open a Wachovia Checking Account as follows. A check for my opening deposit is enclosed. (For your own protection, please do not send cash through the mail.)

Account is to be set up on the following name(s): _____

_____

Sign _____

Sign _____

Mail
Address _____
STREET AND NO.   CITY   STATE   ZIP

Employed by _____
FIRM NAME   POSITION

Social Security No. _____ Date _____

This Account is accepted by Wachovia Bank & Trust Company, N.A., also subject to the provisions stated on the reverse side of this card. Above are the duly authorized signatures which the Bank will recognize in the payment of funds or the transaction of other business.

From *Reading for Survival in Today's Society, Volume One,* © 1978 Goodyear Publishing Company, Inc.

5. COMPLETING A FORM TO OPEN A CHECKING ACCOUNT
Refer to the **checking account form** on page 154 and answer the following:

a. Which part of the form does the person opening the account *not* complete? _____

b. What should you include with the completed checking account form?

_____

c. Complete the form. Decide if one or two names will be on the account. Notice the lines for the person(s) to sign their names and sign your name on one of the lines. Use your address. Decide your "firm name" (employer) and your job title (position) and write those on the appropriate line. Use your social security number or create one, and write today's date.

other ideas
A. Create a banking statement, showing deposits, withdrawals, and a running balance.

B. Using printed information collected from local banks, discuss the different services performed by banks and note the charges for these services.

C. Interview officials of local banks. Compare and contrast advantages and disadvantages of banking services.

D. Develop imaginary households. Using newspaper classified advertisement sections, find a job and an apartment. Using a certain salary as a base, prepare a budget and pay your first month's bills.

E. Write an advertisement suitable for radio broadcast or TV production for one of the banks in your area.

key words & phrases

deposit	account	withdrawal	safe-deposit box
loan	installment	vault	transaction
teller	currency	security	personalized
checking	coin	cashier	service charge
savings	interest	bonds	negotiable

self-evaluation

	date completed	possible score	your score	EXPERT	AVERAGE	FAIR	HELP!
1. Finding the meaning of selected basic words associated with banking		10					
2. Locating the meaning of more complicated banking terms		7					
3. Learning important basic facts about writing checks		6					
4. Noting items on savings withdrawal and deposit slips		12					
5. Completing a form to open a checking account		3					

CIRCLE **other ideas**
COMPLETED: A B C D E

TOTAL POSSIBLE POINTS: **38**

YOUR TOTAL POINTS:

How did you rate yourself?

From Reading for Survival in Today's Society, Volume One, ©1978 Goodyear Publishing Company, Inc.

city information

16

16

CITY INFORMATION

Every community, town, and city has certain characteristics that are unique to it. Some cities are famous for historical or statistical reasons. For example, St. Augustine, Florida, is the nation's oldest city (established in 1565), and New York City is the nation's largest. Many of the nation's smaller cities and towns have become well known because they are the birthplace of a famous person (Independence, Missouri), or the site of an important event (Gettysburg, Pennsylvania). Although much information of this kind is transmitted orally, most cities prepare and distribute printed material—brochures and pamphlets—describing selected public areas and features within their boundaries. One objective of education could well be to develop in each person an awareness of the information printed about the distinguishing features of his or her locale.

Specific reading lessons emphasized in this module are: (1) finding specific information about cities; (2) locating information about shopping centers; (3) using city directories; (4) identifying names and addresses of service companies; and (5) reading specific information about city events.

materials

Encourage students to request copies of other kinds of publications from a city. Examples include Chamber of Commerce materials, information from City Hall, and pamphlets concerning building codes and other restrictions.

[1]Ann Golenpaul, ed., *Information Please Almanac, Atlas and Yearbook 1975* (29th ed.; New York: Simon & Schuster, 1975), p. 629.

survival reading skills

1. FINDING SPECIFIC INFORMATION ABOUT CITIES

Using the information about **Durham, North Carolina**, on page 160, answer the following:

a. After a person moves to Durham from out of state, how many days is his or her automobile driver's license valid? _____

b. How many square miles are there in the county?_____

c. How many motels are there in the Greater Durham area? _____

d. What is the telephone number of the Better Business Bureau?_____

_____

e. What airlines serve Durham? _____

_____

f. What is the telephone number for the intra-city bus service?_____

_____

Using the information about **Denver, Colorado**, on page 161, answer the following:

g. What was Denver's population in 1879?_____

h. What was the 1975 estimate of Denver's population? _____

i. How many square miles are in the city and county? _____

_____

j. By 1910, Denver was the _____

_____ center of the Rocky Mountain region.

k. What two major interstate highways cross in Denver?

(1) _____

(2) _____

Durham, North Carolina

ACCOMMODATIONS
One hotel and 24 motels provide a total of 2,190 rooms in the Greater Durham area. An accommodations directory is available from the Greater Durham Chamber of Commerce.

AIR SERVICE
Raleigh-Durham Airport (RDU), 13 miles southeast of Durham between I-40 and US 70, is North Carolina's second busiest airport. Scheduled service, with almost 50 flights daily, is provided by Delta, Eastern, Piedmont, and United. There are two commuter airlines and charter is available through Raleigh-Durham Aviation and Wheeler Flying Service. Six major firms offer rental cars and limousine service (596-2361) is available to downtown Durham.

AUTO
Driver's Permit: Out-of-state permits are valid for 30 days after North Carolina residency is established. (Out-of-state learner's permits are invalid). For new permits, go to the State Highway Patrol Station on Miami Boulevard. Written, road sign recognition and vision tests are required; a driving test may also be required. The permit fee is $3.25. Permits are good for 4 years, expiring on the birthday. Appointments can be made (596-8284) but are not necessary.

Insurance: Before an auto can be registered in North Carolina, the applicant must show "proof of financial responsibility." Usually, this is done by securing liability insurance coverage and presenting your insurer's certificate when you register and buy plates.

License and Safety Inspection: Out-of-state license plates are valid for 30 days after state residency is established. For new state and city plates, go to Motor Vehicles License Service at Northgate Shopping Center (286-4908). North Carolina requires safety inspection for autos, and this must be done by a licensed service station or garage within 10 days after plates are purchased.

BETTER BUSINESS BUREAU
The Triangle Cities Better Business Bureau serves the Research Triangle Area. Telephone 549-8221 between 9:30 am and 3:30 pm, or visit the office in the Research Triangle Park's Service Center during regular business hours.

BUS SERVICE
Durham has clean and safe intra-city buses operated by Duke Power Company; call 688-4587 for route and schedule information. Carolina Trailways, Central Bus Lines, Continental Trailways, Greyhound Lines and Southern Coach offer scheduled continental service from Union Bus Terminal, Main and Dillard Streets, 682-0405.

GEOGRAPHY
Durham's altitude is 406 feet above sea level. Its geographical coordinates are 36°, 02' North latitude, 78°, 58' West longitude. The area of the city is 38.97 square miles. The county covers 299 square miles.

CHAMBER OF COMMERCE
Founded in 1912, the Greater Durham Chamber of Commerce has a long and proud history of achievement. Through its membership of more than 800 business, professional, and industrial firms, the Chamber is engaged in a broad assortment of programs and activities directed toward improving the economy and livability of the total Durham area. Guide maps and new resident information are available at the office in the Durham Hotel building, Mon.-Fri., 8:30 am-5:00 pm.

CHILD/ ELDERLY CARE
For information on children's day care facilities and nursing and extended care homes for the elderly, check the Yellow Pages or call the Durham County Department of Social Services, 688-6351.

CHURCHES
Durham has over 200 houses of worship representing 41 faiths and denominations. Consult the Yellow Pages.

From *Reading for Survival in Today's Society*, Volume One, ©1978 Goodyear Publishing Company, Inc.

From *Reading for Survival in Today's Society*, Volume One, © 1978 Goodyear Publishing Company, Inc.

Denver, Colorado

By 1879, Denver had a population of 35,000 and boasted the first telephone service in the west. In the 80's and 90's the city experienced another boom — silver. One mining camp after another exploded with prosperity and the wealth found its way to Denver.

When the silver boom ended, Denver settled into a comfortable, respectable prosperity — free of gamblers, drifters and claim jumpers.

By 1910, the city had become the commercial and industrial center of the Rocky Mountain region, with a great cattle market and the largest sheep market in the world. Denver was in the process of becoming the nation's "second capital," with a proliferation of federal offices.

In the years before World War I, Denver gained beauty through the efforts of Mayor Robert Speer. Boulevards and parks were built as well as Civic Center. On a day specified as "Arbor Day" the city gave young trees to all householders who would plant them. And today, Denver continues to have one of the most beautiful park systems of any major metropolitan city.

Since World War II Denver has entered a new era. The skyline has shot up. Population of the metropolitan area is estimated at 1,500,000, ranking it 24th in population in the U.S. (1975, estimate).

Because it has become the distribution center of the Rocky Mountain and High Plains regions, Denver has a highly developed transportation system, Stapleton International Airport. Denver's jet airport facility is the seventh busiest commercial airport in the United States and is served by seven major airlines, several area airlines and various charter services.

Denver is the center of railroad traffic in the Rocky Mountain region because large wholesale and distribution businesses use Denver as a shipping point for distribution of their products. The city also is at the crossroad of two major interstate highways, east-west, I-70 and, north-south, I-25.

The City and County of Denver is a single governmental entity with identical boundaries performing both municipal and county functions and also comprising the Denver Public School District, Denver has a mayor-council form of government with strong executive powers reserved for the mayor. The mayor and councilmen are elected for four-year terms. The most recent municipal election was in 1975. The mayor of Denver is the Honorable William H. McNichols, Jr.

The City and County of Denver is coterminus and has an area of 116.69 square miles.

Denver's Standard Metropolitan Statistical Area (SMSA as defined by the Census Bureau) consists of Adams, Arapahoe, Boulder, Denver, Douglas, Gilpin and Jefferson counties and contains an area of 4,691 square miles.

2. LOCATING INFORMATION ABOUT SHOPPING CENTERS

Using both the **map** on page 164 and the brief information about each shopping center on page 165, answer the following questions:

a. Which shopping center has the largest number of stores, Parkwood Shopping Center or Riverview Shopping Center? _____

_____

b. Which shopping center has the smallest number of stores, College Plaza Shopping Center or Arlans Plaza Shopping Center?_____

_____

c. If you lived on Holloway Street, what would be your nearest shopping center? _____

d. What three shopping centers are on or near Hillsborough Road?

(1) _____

(2) _____

(3) _____

e. If you wanted to go to the largest shopping center near East Club Boulevard, which one would you visit?_____

_____

f. The following abbreviations are used either on the map or in the descriptions of the shopping centers. Write the word or words for which each abbreviation stands.

(1) ST_____

(2) AVE_____

(3) Jr. _____

(4) &_____

(5) BLVD_____

From *Reading for Survival in Today's Society, Volume One,* ©1978 Goodyear Publishing Company, Inc.

(6) E _____

(7) sq. ft. _____

(8) P.O. _____

(9) I-85 _____

(10) RD _____

3. USING CITY DIRECTORIES

Locate the telephone directory listing for your city. Make a chart listing ten major offices, such as tax collector, mayor, registrar of deeds, and the like. On the chart, write at least one service performed in each office. Request information by writing letters or making telephone calls to offices if you do not know their services. Discuss the various kinds of jobs performed at the city government level.

4. IDENTIFYING NAMES AND ADDRESSES OF SERVICE COMPANIES

Residents in each geographical location use a certain mailing address and telephone number to correspond with electric, gas, water, sewer, and telephone companies or agencies. Using either bills from these companies or the telephone directory, write the information below.

	ADDRESS	TELEPHONE
Electric Company		
Gas Company		
Water Department		
Sewer Department		
Telephone Company		

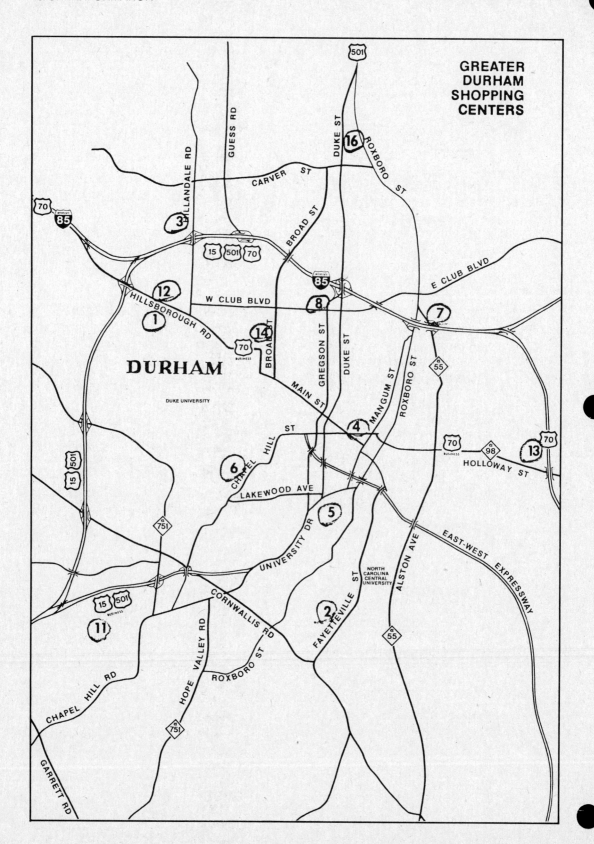

GREATER
DURHAM
SHOPPING
CENTERS

From *Reading for Survival in Today's Society*, Volume One, © 1978 Goodyear Publishing Company, Inc.

1. ARLANS PLAZA SHOPPING CENTER - 3300 Hillsborough Road (Mrs. Dottie Smithwick, P. O. Box 24241, Ft. Lauderdale, Florida 33307) 85,000 sq. ft.; 7 stores or services in operation. Parking area for 200 cars.

2. COLLEGE PLAZA SHOPPING CENTER - 3000 Fayetteville Street (Fred Stell, Allenton Realty, Orange Street, phone: 688-4355) 21,500 sq. ft.; 5 stores or services in operation. Parking area for 200 cars.

3. CROASDAILE SHOPPING CENTER - 1821 Hillandale Road (B. T. Associates, 1821 Hillandale Road, phone: 383-1502) 68,500 sq. ft.; 12 stores or services in operation. Parking area for 600 cars.

4. DOWNTOWN DURHAM - Main Street (Downtown Foundation, P. O. Box 610, phone: 682-9241) 931,512 sq. ft.; 140 stores or services in operation. Parking area for 3,340 cars.

5. FOREST HILLS SHOPPING CENTER - University Drive (A. Y. Alexander, P. O. Box 8656, Forest Hills Station) 43,500 sq. ft.; 16 stores or services in operation. Parking area for 275 cars.

6. LAKEWOOD SHOPPING CENTER - 2000 Chapel Hill St. (Randolph R. Few, 1502 Moreland Avenue, phone: 489-7805) 250,000 sq. ft.; 34 stores or services in operation. Parking area for 2,000 cars.

7. MURDOCK SHOPPING CENTER - Avondale & I-85 (Bill Murdock, P. O. Box 866, phone: 682-2169) 121,000 sq. ft.; 2 stores in operation. Parking area for 1500 cars.

8. NORTHGATE SHOPPING CENTER - West Club Blvd. at Gregson Street (Kenan Rand, Jr., Office Area 2, Room 200, phone: 286-4407) 800,000 sq. ft.; 100 stores or services in operation. Parking area for 3,500 cars.

9. PARKWOOD SHOPPING CENTER - N. C. 54 in Parkwood (Key Homes, 1413 Seaton Road, phone: 544-1702) 17,700 sq. ft.; 8 stores or services in operation. Parking area for 250 cars.

10. RIVERVIEW SHOPPING CENTER - U. S. 501, Roxboro Road (Jerry M. Pierce, P. O. Box 12684, Charlotte, N. C. 28205, phone: (704) 525-7394 125,000 sq. ft.; 24 stores or services in operation. Parking area for 750 cars.

11. SOUTH SQUARE SHOPPING CENTER - 3400 Hillsborough Road (Plaza Associates, Chapel Hill Blvd., phone: 493-1441) 855,272 sq. ft. under construction 103 stores or services when completed. Parking area for 4,500 cars

12. UNIVERSITY SHOPPING CENTER - 3400 Hillsborough Road (Eric Tilley, Jr., P. O. Box 3037, phone: 383-3711) 100,000 sq. ft.; 8 stores or services in operation. Parking area for 500 cars.

13. WELLONS VILLAGE SHOPPING CENTER - S. Miami Blvd. & Holloway Street (Joe Jernigan, P. O. Box 11056, East Durham Station, phone: 682-8000) 230,000 sq. ft.; 48 stores or services in operation. Parking area for 1500 cars.

14. WESTFIELD SHOPPING CENTER - Broad Street & West Main (Mr. D. H. Norris, P. O. Box 2537, West Durham Station, phone: 383-1596) 35,000 sq. ft.; 8 stores or services in operation. Parking area for 250 cars.

15. WILLOW PARK MALL - Chapel Hill Blvd. (15-501 South) (Mrs. L. H. Rhew, 4422 Chapel Hill Blvd., phone: 489-1305) 23,000 sq. ft.; 20 stores or services in operation. Parking area for 150 cars.

16. NORTH DUKE MALL - 3600 North Duke Street (North Duke Mall, Ltd. Partnership, P. O. Box 1107, phone: 682-0855) 186,000 sq. ft.; under construction, 45 stores or services when completed. Parking area for 960 cars.

9/17/74

5. READING SPECIFIC INFORMATION ABOUT CITY EVENTS
Using articles in a local newspaper, locate city-based information about each of the following and write one main point about each in the space below:

A PERSON _____

_____

_____

A PLACE _____

_____

_____

SOMETHING NEW _____

_____

_____

SOMETHING OLD _____

_____

_____

other ideas

A. Prepare a list of the names and positions of each *elected* city official.

B. Make a time line of the major events in your town's history, from its original founding to the present. Illustrate the time line.

C. Using the index of a city map, circle all of the streets or other sites named for *people*. See if you can discover why these people were so honored.

D. Invite a city official to speak to the class concerning the services of the agency or office represented by that person.

E. Compare the agencies in your city government with those in another town. Are there services your town should offer but does not?

From *Reading for Survival in Today's Society*, Volume One, ©1978 Goodyear Publishing Company, Inc.

key words & phrases

municipal	official	street	custodian
commerce	mayor	parking	water treatment
urban	city hall	fire	police
merchant	assessment	library	sanitation
public	school	planning	comptroller

self-evaluation

	date completed	possible score	your score	EXPERT	AVERAGE	FAIR	HELP!
1. Finding specific information about cities		**12**					
2. Locating information about shopping centers		**17**					
3. Using city directories		**20**					
4. Identifying names and addresses of service companies		**10**					
5. Reading specific information about city events		**4**					

CIRCLE **other ideas**
COMPLETED: A B C D E

TOTAL POSSIBLE POINTS: **63**

YOUR TOTAL POINTS:

How did you rate yourself?

state government information

17

17

STATE GOVERNMENT INFORMATION

As a public service that is supported by public funds, each state prints and disseminates a variety of information each year. Much of this information is free or inexpensive. Possible sources of such information include state agencies, for example, those dealing with agriculture, employment, education, transportation, government, public health, revenue, and recreation. Students should become aware of these kinds of materials and learn how to obtain and read them.

Specific reading lessons emphasized in this module are: (1) learning selected words associated with taxes; (2) completing a mock individual income tax return; (3) finding specific information about taxes; (4) understanding steps in enacting state legislation; and (5) reading state safety publications.

materials

Encourage students to write to various state agencies requesting general information about literature provided at little or no cost. Once they know what is available, students should write for information of interest to them.

survival reading skills

1. LEARNING SELECTED WORDS ASSOCIATED WITH TAXES

Using information in this module, or the dictionary if necessary, write the meaning of the following words as they relate to taxation.

a. exemption _____

_____

b. dependent _____

_____

c. estate _____

_____

d. deduction _____

_____

e. resident _____

_____

f. contribution _____

_____

g. gross income _____

_____

2. COMPLETING A MOCK INDIVIDUAL INCOME TAX RETURN

Pretend you have been asked to complete the **state individual income tax return** on pages 173 and 174 for a friend. Here is all the information given to you:

Friend's name: Katherine Vann Williams
Street address: 1289 Pare Street
City, state, and zip code: Austin, Texas, 78723
Occupation: Construction Worker
Social security number: 898-38-8564
Marital status: Widow
Children: Benjamin David Williams, age 12, IQ over 40
　　　　　(no other dependents)
Present employer: Drake Construction Company
Wages: $23,343.85 (no other income)
Business-connected deductions: $589.87

a. What other information do you need to complete the form?

(1) _____

_____

(2) _____

_____

(3) _____

_____

(4) _____

_____

(5) _____

b. There are two places on the form to write the date. Where are they?

(1) _____

(2) _____

3. FINDING SPECIFIC INFORMATION ABOUT TAXES

Use the **Personal Exemption** information on page 175 to complete the following statements:

a. A blind individual may claim $_____ as an additional tax exemption.

b. A person over 65 years old may claim $_____ as an additional tax exemption.

c. Each head of a household may claim a $_____ exemption.

d. Each qualified dependent is entitled to a $_____ exemption.

e. Name three examples of institutions of higher learning persons may attend as dependents.

(1) _____

(2) _____

(3) _____

f. To have a household, a person must live in the same place

_____ days or more during the year.

NORTH CAROLINA
INDIVIDUAL INCOME TAX RETURN

for filing a combined husband and wife, separate, or single return, resident or nonresident

1975

or other taxable year beginning _ _ _ _ _ _ _ _ _.1975, ending _ _ _ _ _ _ _ _19_ _

DUE APRIL 15, 1976

Make check payable to and mail to N.C. DEPT. of REVENUE, P.O. Box 25000, Raleigh, N.C. 27640.

If a refund is due, mail to N.C. DEPT. of REVENUE, P.O. Box R, Raleigh, N.C. 27634.

Please Print or Type

NAME (first names and initials of both, if combined) | LAST NAME | Your Soc. Sec. No.

NUMBER AND STREET, including apartment number or rural route

CITY, TOWN, OR POST OFFICE, STATE, AND ZIP CODE | COUNTY OF RESIDENCE

Wife's Soc. Sec. No.

Your Occupation | Wife's Occupation | DO NOT WRITE IN THIS SPACE

If this is a separate form, give your wife's (or husband's) name _____ gross income _____ and S.S. No. _____

Did you file a 1974 N.C. return? Husband or Single Yes ☐ No ☐; Wife Yes ☐ No ☐ If either answer is No, state reason _____

Were you a legal resident of N.C. during the entire year of 1975? Husband or Single Yes ☐ No ☐; Wife Yes ☐ No ☐ If either answer is No, complete separate Schedule A

PERSONAL EXEMPTION — See instructions and check the blocks that apply	a Husband or Single	b Wife
1 ☐ Single or ☐ other individual not claiming $2,000 exemption . . . . Enter $1,000		
2a. ☐ Married living with spouse, and claiming $2,000 exemption		
b. ☐ Divorced having custody of a child under 18 & receiving no alimony or support . . } Enter		
c. ☐ Single, ☐ widow, widower, ☐ or divorced person maintaining a household . . . } $2,000 . . .		
d. ☐ Widow or widower, having a child under 18, ☐ Other (Attach explanation) . . .		
3. ☐ 65 or over, ☐ blind . . . . Enter $1,000 for each box checked		
4a. ☐ First names of your dependent children who lived with you _____ Enter $600 for each . . .		
(attach an explanation for each claimed dependent child by a previous marriage)		
b. ☐ $600 for each other dependent from reverse		
c. ☐ Additional $600 for each dependent in an institution of higher learning		
☐ Additional $2,000 for each dependent with an I.Q. under 40. Attach statement		
TOTAL ALLOWABLE PERSONAL EXEMPTION (carry to line 14 or Schedule A)		

Your (or husband's) present employer: _____ Address _____
Wife's present employer: _____ Address _____

		a	b
7. Wages, salaries, tips, etc. — attach explanation if not shown on wage and tax statement.	7.		
8. Other income (or loss) — From page 2, Part I, line 7	8.		
9. TOTAL INCOME — Total of lines 7 and 8	9.		
10. Subtract business connected deductions (from page 2, Part II)	10.		
11. ADJUSTED GROSS INCOME (Subtract line 10 from line 9)	11.		
12. Nonbusiness deductions from page 2, Part III, line 7, or STANDARD DEDUCTION — 10% of line 11 ($500 maximum) or from separate Schedule A, Part III, line 4, if prorated.	12.		
13. Subtract line 12 from line 11	13.		
14. PERSONAL EXEMPTION (from line 6 or from separate Schedule A, Part II, line 7)	14.		
15. NET TAXABLE INCOME (Subtract line 14 from line 13)	15.		
16. AMOUNT OF TAX — Use the schedule on reverse (page 2) of this return	16.		
16a. Total of Columns a. plus b. on line 16 — This is your COMBINED TAX LIABILITY	16a.		
17. a. N. C. Tax Withheld (Attach State copy of each wage and tax statement)	17a.		
b. Payments on 1975 declaration of estimated tax	b.		
c. Credit for income tax paid another state (from separate Schedule A)	c.		
18. Enter TOTAL of lines 17, a, b, c	18.		
19. If line 16a., is more than line 18., enter . . . . BALANCE DUE	19.		
20. If line 16a., is less than line 18., enter . . . . AMOUNT TO BE REFUNDED	20.		

N. C. ELECTION CAMPAIGN FUND

If you wish to designate $1.00 to this fund, enter name of Party _____

If your spouse (if combined) wishes to designate $1.00 to this fund, enter name of Party _____

Signature ▶ | Your signature | Date

Under penalties prescribed by law, I hereby affirm that to the best of my knowledge and belief this return, including any accompanying schedules and statements, is true and complete. If prepared by a person other than taxpayer, his affirmation is based on all information of which he has any knowledge

Spouse's signature (if filing combined return, both must sign) | ▶ Preparer's signature (other than taxpayer) | Date

Do not write in this space

TAX _____ PEN _____ INT _____ TOT _____ CR _____ BAL _____

Other Dependents	(a) NAME (If filing combined. indicate wife by W, husband by H.)	(b) Relationship	(c) Months lived in your home. If born or died during year, write B or D.	(d) Did dependent have income of $1,000 or more ?	(e) Amount YOU furnished for dependent's support. If 100% write ALL.	(f) Amount furnished by OTHERS including dependent
	Total number listed in column (a) for wife		for husband or single			

PART I. INCOME FROM SOURCES OTHER THAN WAGES, SALARIES, ETC.

DIVIDENDS	Name of Corp.	(a)%Taxable	(b) Total dividends received	
			Husband or Single	Wife

1. Total Dividends . . . . ▶

INTEREST INCOME Exclusive of N. C. and U. S. obligations. Include interest credited to your account.

Interest includes earnings from savings and loan associations, mutual savings banks, cooperative banks, and credit unions as well as interest on bank deposits, bonds, tax refunds, etc.

Names of Payers:

2. Total interest income . . . .

OTHER INCOME (Attach appropriate schedules)

3. Pensions and annuities, gains (or losses) rents or royalties, partnerships, estates and trusts, alimony, etc. (from Schedule B) . . . .

4. Business Income (from Schedule C) .

5. Farm Income (from Schedule F) . . .

Miscellaneous income (identify):

6. Total Miscellaneous income . . . ▶

7. TOTAL (add lines 1 through 6)
Enter here and on page 1, line 8 . . ▶

PART II. BUSINESS CONNECTED DEDUCTIONS

(See instructions)	Husband or Single	Wife
From separate Schedule E		
Other (identify):		
TOTAL Carry to page 1, line 10 . . ▶		

TAX RATES

If Net Taxable Income Is:
Not over $2,000 . . . . 3% of net taxable income.

Over	but not over	The Tax Is:	of amt. over
$2,000	$4,000	$ 60 + 4%	$2,000.
$4,000	$6,000	$140 + 5%	$4,000.
$6,000	$10,000	$240 + 6%	$6,000.
$10,000		$480 + 7%	$10,000.

PART III. ITEMIZED NONBUSINESS DEDUCTIONS Do not complete this Part, if you or your spouse claim standard deduction

	(c) Taxable (Column (a) times Column (b))		(d) Deductible (Column (b) minus Column (c))	
	Husband or Single	Wife	Husband or Single	Wife

1. Deductible Dividends . . . . . ▶

MEDICAL EXPENSES (Enter amount not compensated by insurance or otherwise)

Medicine and drugs . . . .

Doctors, dentists, etc. . . . .

Hospitals . . . .

Other (itemize):

Total . . . . ▶

Less 5% of line 11, page 1 . . . . .

2. Allowable med. expense . . . ▶

CONTRIBUTIONS

For which you have receipts, etc.

List other

3. Total (Not over 15% of line 11, page 1)

TAXES (Income, gasoline, sales, inheritance, or gift taxes not deductible)

City and county property . . . . .

Telephone tax . . . .

4. TOTAL . . . . ▶

INTEREST PAID Home mortgage .

Other

5. TOTAL . . . . ▶

MISCELLANEOUS Identify

Child care (attach D-442) . . . . .

6. Total . . . . ▶

7. TOTAL DEDUCTIONS (add lines 1 through 6)- Carry to page 1, line 12 . . . ▶

From *Reading for Survival in Today's Society*, Volume One, ©1978 Goodyear Publishing Company, Inc.

PERSONAL EXEMPTION

(These exemptions are for individuals reporting all income to North Carolina. An individual reporting only a portion of his income to North Carolina is required to prorate his exemption as explained under "Prorating Personal Exemption.")

Single Person or Married Woman

A single person not qualifying for the head of household exemption or a married woman with a separate income is allowed a personal exemption of $1,000.

Married Man Living With Wife

A married-man living with his wife is allowed a $2,000 personal exemption. If the wife has an income and is required to file a return, she is entitled to a $1,000 personal exemption on her return, and her husband is still entitled to a $2,000 exemption. A full year's exemption of $2,000 is allowed to a married man if his wife dies or if he marries during the taxable year. A married man may not claim an additional $600 dependency exemption for his wife.

Married Woman Claiming Husband's Exemption

A married woman living with her husband may, by agreement with him, claim his $2,000 exemption if the husband files a return and claims a $1,000 exemption regardless of whether or not he has any reportable income. A married woman cannot claim a $600 dependency exemption for her husband.

Head of Household

A $2,000 head of household exemption may be claimed by a single individual, a widow, a widower, or a divorced individual who maintains a household which constitutes the principal place of abode for himself, herself, or his or her closely related dependent, if the following conditions are met:

1. The individual must have provided more than half the cost of maintaining the household for the year.
2. The household must have been the principal place of abode for the individual or his or her closely related dependent for 183 days or more during the year.
3. The household must have been a place of abode having those facilities normally required for both eating and sleeping.

A "closely related dependent" is one for whom a $600 dependency exemption is allowable. The head of household exemption, which is in lieu of all other basic exemptions, may not be claimed by two individuals in the same household.

One who ceases to be a head of household but qualified as head of household for the major portion of a year may claim the $2,000 exemption for that year.

Divorced or Separated Individuals

A husband and wife who are separated with the intent to remain separate and apart (estranged) are considered to be "divorced individuals" for income tax purposes.

A divorced individual having custody of a minor child or children (under 18 years of age) and receiving neither alimony nor support payments for the child or children may claim a $2,000 personal exemption. A divorced individual furnishing major support for a child may be entitled to claim a $600 dependency exemption (see "Dependents" below) irrespective of whether the individual has custody of the child or qualifies for a $2,000 exemption. A divorced parent having custody of a child but not furnishing chief support for the child may not claim a $600 dependency exemption for that child. A basic personal exemption of only $1,000 is allowable to a divorced individual who does not have custody of a minor child, even though supporting the child unless he or she can qualify as head of household.

Widow or Widower

A widow or widower having a minor child (a child under 18 years of age) may claim the widow's or widower's exemption of $2,000, whether or not the minor child receives his support from that individual. If the minor child does receive chief support and qualifies as a dependent, the $600 dependency exemption will be allowed. A widow or widower not having a minor child or other allowable dependents is entitled to only a $1,000 personal exemption unless he or she can qualify for the head of household exemption.

Blind Individual

An additional exemption of $1,000 may be claimed by one who is blind if a supporting statement is attached to the return. This applies only to the taxpayer and not to the wife, husband or dependent.

Individual Age 65 or Over

An additional exemption of $1,000 may be claimed by one who has reached the age of 65 years on or before the last day of the taxable year. This exemption applies only to the taxpayer and not the wife, husband, or dependents of the taxpayer.

Individual With Retarded Dependent

An additional exemption of $2,000 may be claimed for a dependent with an Intelligence Quotient under 40 if a supporting statement from a licensed psychologist or physician showing that the I. Q. is under 40 is attached.

Fiduciary

A fiduciary filing a return for a minor or for an incompetent individual should claim the personal exemption to which the individual is entitled.

A fiduciary filing a return for one who has died during the year may claim the basic $1,000 or $2,000 exemption to which the individual would have been entitled while living.

Dependents

In addition to the basic exemption of $1,000 or $2,000, a deduction of $600 may be claimed for each qualified dependent. To claim an individual as a dependent the following three tests must be met:

1. Over one-half of the support for the year must be furnished by the taxpayer. (See reference to multiple support declaration below.)
2. The income of the individual claimed must be less than $1,000 during the year (except a child or stepchild of the taxpayer who was a full-time student or under 19 years of age).
3. The individual must fall within one of the following classes:
   (a) Related to the taxpayer as follows: son, daughter, stepchild, mother, father, grandparent, brother, sister, grandchild, stepbrother, stepsister, stepmother, stepfather, mother-in-law, father-in-law, brother-in-law, sister-in-law, son-in-law, daughter-in-law; and the following if related by blood: aunt, uncle, nephew, niece.
   (b) A member of the same household as the taxpayer.
   (c) A former member of the same household as the taxpayer receiving institutional care because of a mental or physical disability.

Children of a marriage may be claimed only by the spouse claiming the $2,000 exemption, except that a child by a previous marriage, or by divorced parents may be claimed by the one furnishing chief support. One claiming a child by a previous marriage should attach a statement to the return explaining that the child is by a previous marriage.

Neither a husband nor a wife may under any circumstances claim the other as a dependent.

When the support contributed by several persons constitutes the chief support for an individual during the year but no one person contributes over 50%, the chief support of a dependent (other than son, daughter, stepson, or stepdaughter of the taxpayer) is treated as received from the taxpayer if he provides over 10% and if he attaches to his return a Form D-433A, Multiple Support Declaration (available at offices listed on page 1), signed by others contributing over 10%.

Dependents in Institution of Higher Learning

An additional exemption of $600 may be claimed for each dependent who is a full-time student on the last day of the income year or for at least five months during the year at an accredited college or university, a business college, a beauty school, a barber college, a technical institute, a nurses school, or other institution of higher learning for purposes other than to secure a high school diploma. This additional exemption may not be claimed by a taxpayer for himself, herself, or for husband or wife.

Prorating Personal Exemption

The following individuals are required by North Carolina Statutes to prorate their personal exemptions:

1. A nonresident for the entire year having income both within and outside North Carolina.
2. A new resident who has lived in North Carolina only for a part of the year.
3. A former resident who moved from North Carolina during the year.

The prorated exemption must be determined by completing Part II of separate Schedule A. When filing a combined return, attach separate schedules for each spouse if required.

Miscellaneous Information

The status on the last day of the income year determines the right to the exemptions described above, except that: 1. One is entitled to claim dependents who died during the income year;

4. UNDERSTANDING STEPS IN ENACTING STATE LEGISLATION
Refer to the **Steps in Enacting a House Bill in the Oregon Legislative Assembly** on page 177 and answer the following:

a. Where is the bill first introduced?_____

_____

b. List three steps that follow the bill's introduction.

(1) _____

(2) _____

(3) _____

c. If the bill passes the House, it goes to the _____

_____

d. How many readings does the bill get after it passes the House? _____

e. If the bill passes the Senate, it goes to the _____

_____

f. Write two things that might happen to the bill after it goes back to the House.

(1) _____

(2) _____

g. What is one thing the governor must do before a bill can become a law?

_____

_____

h. In Oregon, where could you find a copy of all bills that have become law?

_____

_____

STEPS IN ENACTING A HOUSE BILL

IN THE OREGON LEGISLATIVE ASSEMBLY

Bill introduced

IN THE HOUSE:

PRESENTATION
Typed bill presented to Chief Clerk who sends it to Engrossing & Enrolling section to be checked for form and style. It is then returned to Chief Clerk for

INTRODUCTION
and sent to the State Printer for printing. It is then placed on the calendar for

FIRST READING
(title only)
and

SECOND READING
(title only)
and referred to a standing committee for

STANDING COMMITTEE CONSIDERATION

Consideration	Report
Committee may:	(usually)
1. Hold hearings.	1. Do Pass.
2. Table bill.	2. Do Pass with Amendments.
3. Report bill from committee.	3. Majority and Minority.
4. Hold bill and report substitute.	

ENGROSSMENT
If report was "Do Pass with Amendments," amendments are engrossed into printed bill by Engrossing and Enrolling section. Bill as engrossed may be printed.

THIRD READING
Section by section unless waived by ⅔ vote.

VOTING
After debate, bill may be:
1. Returned to committee.
2. Amended on floor by unanimous consent.
3. Passed or rejected. (An adverse vote may be reconsidered)

If bill passes House it goes

TO THE SENATE:

FIRST READING

SECOND READING

STANDING COMMITTEE CONSIDERATION

ENGROSSMENT
(if amended)

THIRD READING

VOTING

If bill passes Senate it is returned

TO THE HOUSE:

IF:
Bill passes Senate without amendment it is returned to House for enrollment.

BUT

IF:
Bill passes Senate with amendment it is returned to House for further consideration.

IF:
House accepts Senate amendment the bill is enrolled

BUT

IF:
House rejects Senate amendment the bill is sent to a Conference Committee for

CONFERENCE COMMITTEE CONSIDERATION

The Committee	Report
1. Consists of members of both Houses.	1. Recommends compromise.
2. Attempts to resolve differences.	2. States inability to resolve differences.

IF:
Both houses accept Conference Committee compromise the bill is enrolled

BUT

IF:
One or both houses reject Conference Committee compromise and new committees are chosen and fail, bill fails.

OR

IF:
Conference Committee states inability to resolve differences and new committees are chosen and fail, bill fails.

ENROLLMENT
Amendments (if any) are engrossed in bill which is then prepared for enrollment and sent to State Printer for printing.

SIGNATURES
The enrolled bill is signed by Speaker of House and President of Senate and is sent to Governor.

Enrolled bill

ENACTED INTO LAW:

GOVERNOR

Enrolled bill becomes law if:

1. Governor signs.
2. Fails to sign but does not veto.
3. Both houses pass over Governor's veto (2/3 vote).
4. Bill is referred to people who approve at election.

SECRETARY OF STATE

Enrolled Act filed with Secretary of State.

It is given a chapter number and included in biennial compilation known as SESSION LAWS.

LEGISLATIVE COUNSEL

Enrolled Act is inserted in appropriate place or places in latest edition of OREGON REVISED STATUTES.

PREPARED BY LEGISLATIVE COUNSEL COMMITTEE

5. READING STATE SAFETY PUBLICATIONS

All states publish safety requirements, not only for automobiles but also for other types of motor vehicles. Use the state of Idaho publication concerning **motorcycles** on page 179 to answer the following questions:

a. Write your own definition of the term *motorcycle* in 20 words or less.

_____

_____

Compare your definition with the one used by the state of Idaho.

b. What types of vehicles are excluded in Idaho's definition? _____

_____

c. What is the maximum number of persons allowed to ride on a motorcycle

at one time?_____

d. Skim the article to find the most important safety requirement concerning

motorcycles. Summarize this requirement. _____

_____

_____

_____

e. Are motorcycle passengers required to wear safety helmets? _____

_____

f. Compare the motorcycle safety requirements of Idaho with those of your state.

(1) What are the similarities? _____

_____

_____

_____

From *Reading for Survival in Today's Society*, Volume One, ©1978 Goodyear Publishing Company, Inc.

(2) What are the differences? _____

_____

_____

_____

Motorcycles

49-761. Riding on motorcycles. A person operating a motorcycle shall ride only upon the permanent and regular seat attached thereto, and such operator shall not carry any other person nor shall any other person ride on a motorcycle unless such motorcycle is designed to carry more than one person, in which event a passenger may ride upon the permanent and regular seat if designed for two (2) persons, or upon another seat firmly attached to the rear or side of the operator. [1953, ch. 273, § 114, p. 478.]

49-761A. Motorcycle safety helmets—Requirements and standards. (a) No person shall ride upon a motorcycle as operator or passenger, upon any public road or highway, unless at all times when so operating or riding upon said vehicle he is wearing, as part of his motorcycle equipment, a protective safety helmet of a type and quality equal to or better than the standards established for such helmets by the director.

(b) "Motorcycle" as used in this section shall mean every motor vehicle designed to travel on not more than three (3) wheels in contact with the ground, except any such motor vehicle as may be included within the term "tractor" as defined by chapter 1, title 49, Idaho Code.

(c) The director is hereby authorized to adopt and publish rules and regulations establishing reasonable standards for such safety helmets. [I. C., § 49-761A, as added by 1967, ch. 224, § 1, p. 675; am. 1974, ch. 27, § 128, p. 931.]

---

other ideas

A. Create a tourist bulletin designed to "advertise" your state as perfect either for vacations or for business development. How does the emphasis differ?

B. With a group of students, send a postcard to each state's tourist bureau requesting one specific type of information, such as information about recreation facilities or state history. Compare the types and amounts of information sent by each state. An almanac would be a good resource for finding correct addresses.

C. As head of the State Department of Agriculture, you must disseminate information about the foods produced in your state. Design a bulletin that describes the top ten food items produced. For example:

Over one million gallons of milk produced in 1976. Southwestern part of the state is primary dairy area.

Create a symbol for each food product.

D. Using a yearly almanac, locate the vital statistics concerning your state. These statistics might include facts relating to the population, number of cars, number of cities with a population over 100,000, and so forth. Put these figures in easy-reading form on a chart, graph, or table.

E. Use the table developed in Activity D to make up mathematics problems about your state. For example: If the population = X, and the number of telephones = Y, how many telephones are there in the state per person? (**Hint:** $Y \div X$ = number of telephones per person.)

F. Role play a meeting of representatives of different government agencies. The purpose of the meeting is to discuss ways to improve coordination among the agencies represented.

G. Design a brochure to be used by one state agency.

H. Write one of your state senators and request information concerning education laws, state appropriations for education, and how he or she stands on the matter of teacher salary raises. Letters from other students might be mailed to the governor, lieutenant governor, representatives, and other senators. Compare the information received.

I. Look through several issues of the newspaper and locate at least three articles that have a dateline from the state capital or were written about events that occurred there. Paste the articles in the space below, then write one cause and one effect for the event described in each.

key words & phrases

taxes	funds	development	governor
park	county	reconstruct	secondary road
law	district	commission	historical site
audit	survey	employee	agency
page	budget	compromise	department

From Reading for Survival in Today's Society, Volume One, ©1978 Goodyear Publishing Company, Inc.

self-evaluation

	date completed	possible score	your score	EXPERT	AVERAGE	FAIR	HELP!
1. Learning selected words associated with taxes		**7**					
2. Completing a mock individual income tax return		**5**					
3. Finding specific information about taxes		**8**					
4. Understanding steps in enacting state legislation		**11**					
5. Reading state safety publications		**7**					

CIRCLE **other ideas**
COMPLETED: A B C D E
                    F G H I

TOTAL POSSIBLE POINTS:
36

YOUR TOTAL POINTS:

How did you rate yourself?

name & date

From *Reading for Survival in Today's Society*, Volume One, ©1978 Goodyear Publishing Company, Inc.

national government information

18

18

NATIONAL GOVERNMENT INFORMATION

The United States Government Printing Office publishes a tremendous number of publications each year. It is not unusual for one who writes a government agency in Washington requesting information to receive, in addition to the specific material requested, a brochure listing available publications on the same and related topics. These publications are most frequently free or inexpensive. Also coming from the nation's capital are news releases and reports from elected senators and representatives. Students should be made aware of the variety of printed information disseminated from Washington, D.C., and they should be helped in reading such material.

Specific reading lessons emphasized in this module are: (1) locating nearest regional address to request government information; (2) noting directions to request government material; (3) finding reports of government decisions; (4) identifying key information on a social security card application form; and (5) reading information on $1.00, $5.00, and $10.00 bills.

materials

Encourage students to write different national government agencies requesting free materials related to a study topic. Suggest they write their state's congressional representatives and ask to receive information sent to constituents.

From *Reading for Survival in Today's Society,* Volume One, ©1978 Goodyear Publishing Company, Inc.

survival reading skills

1. LOCATING NEAREST REGIONAL ADDRESS TO REQUEST GOVERNMENT INFORMATION

Refer to the April, 1976, **United States Department of Agriculture** information concerning the list of publications on page 187 and answer the following:

a. In what city and state is the regional office nearest you? _____

_____

b. In what city and state is the regional office nearest you if you live in Oklahoma or Arkansas? _____

c. In what city and state is the regional office nearest you if you live in Maine or Vermont? _____

d. What is the first line of the address of the main office in Washington, D.C.?_____

e. What is the street and room address of the Dallas, Texas, regional office?

(1) Street _____

(2) Room _____

2. NOTING DIRECTIONS TO REQUEST GOVERNMENT MATERIAL

Refer to the April, 1976, USDA's **Food and Nutrition Service** information on page 187 and answer the following:

a. If you order material that has a cost, where do you mail the order?

_____

_____

_____

b. Is there a cost if you order one copy? _____

_____

c. Look at the first paragraph under the heading "Free Publications." What two things should you write when requesting some of this material?

(1) _____

(2) _____

d. Look at the second paragraph under the heading "Free Publications." What two things should you include in your request to identify this material?

(1) _____

(2) _____

3. FINDING REPORTS OF GOVERNMENT DECISIONS

Locate newspaper articles about decisions made by the congress or the president in Washington, D.C. Below, list at least three of these decisions, why they were made, and the name of at least one person who reported each decision.

DECISION _____

_____

REASON(S) FOR DECISION _____

_____

_____

NAMES_____

_____

DECISION _____

_____

REASON(S) FOR DECISION _____

_____

_____

NAMES_____

_____

DECISION _____

_____

REASON(S) FOR DECISION _____

_____

NAMES_____

April 1976

Current list of Publications of the USDA's Food and Nutrition Service

An illustrated and descriptive list, FNS-11 will be distributed in the near future.

FREE PUBLICATIONS

Single copies of FNS publications are available free, unless a price is given after the description. Requests for publications in quantity must be accompanied by an explanation of the need for the materials and how they will be used in support of food assistance programs.

Requests--giving both the title and the series-number of publications needed--should be addressed to the nearest Food and Nutrition Service Regional office:

U.S. Department of Agriculture
Food and Nutrition Service
Northwest Park
34 Third Avenue
Burlington, Massachusetts 01803

U.S. Department of Agriculture
Food and Nutrition Service
729 Alexander Road
Princeton, New Jersey 08550

U.S. Department of Agriculture
Food and Nutrition Service
1100 Spring Street, N.W., Room 200
Atlanta, Georgia 30309

U.S. Department of Agriculture
Food and Nutrition Service
536 South Clark Street
Chicago, Illinois 60605

U.S. Department of Agriculture
Food and Nutrition Service
1100 Commerce Street, Room 5-D-22
Dallas, Texas 75242

U.S. Department of Agriculture
Food and Nutrition Service
550 Kearny Street
San Francisco, California 94108

or to the

Information Division
U.S. Department of Agriculture
Food and Nutrition Service
Washington, D.C. 20250

SALE PUBLICATIONS

Those publications which have a price listed after the description are free only to cooperators in FNS programs. Others may send orders for those "sale only" materials, giving the title and the series-number, and enclosing payment to:

Superintendent of Documents, U.S. Government Printing Office,
Washington, D.C. 20402

4. IDENTIFYING KEY INFORMATION ON A SOCIAL SECURITY CARD APPLICATION FORM

Discuss specialized words on a social security card application form. Read the instructions for completing it, and then fill it out. Locate the address of the social security office nearest you. If you do not have a social security card, mail or take your application to that office. Discuss the purpose and function of the social security system.

ID: **CN:**   **DO:**

APPLICATION FOR A SOCIAL SECURITY NUMBER

⎣DO NOT WRITE IN THE ABOVE SPACE⎦

See Instructions on Back.   Print in Black or Dark Blue Ink or Use Typewriter.

1 Print FULL NAME YOU WILL USE IN WORK OR BUSINESS	*(First Name)* *(Middle Name or Initial—if none, draw line ____)*	*(Last Name)*
2 Print FULL NAME GIVEN YOU AT BIRTH		**6** YOUR DATE OF BIRTH *(Month) (Day) (Year)*
3 PLACE OF BIRTH *(City)* *(County if known)* *(State)*		**7** YOUR PRESENT AGE *(Age on last birthday)*
4 MOTHER'S FULL NAME AT HER BIRTH *(Her maiden name)*		**8** YOUR SEX MALE ☐ FEMALE ☐
5 FATHER'S FULL NAME *(Regardless of whether living or dead)*		**9** YOUR COLOR OR RACE WHITE ☐ NEGRO ☐ OTHER ☐

10 HAVE YOU EVER BEFORE APPLIED FOR OR HAD A UNITED STATES SOCIAL SECURITY, RAILROAD, OR TAX ACCOUNT NUMBER?   NO ☐   DON'T KNOW ☐   YES ☐   (If "Yes" Print **State** in which you applied and **Date** you applied and **Social Security Number** if known)

11 YOUR MAILING ADDRESS *(Number and Street, Apt. No., P.O. Box, or Rural Route)*   *(City)*   *(State)*   *(Zip Code)*

12 TODAY'S DATE

NOTICE Whoever, with intent to falsify his or someone else's true identity, willfully furnishes or causes to be furnished false information in applying for a social security number, is subject to a fine of not more than $1,000 or imprisonment for up to 1 year, or both.

13 TELEPHONE NUMBER   **14** Sign YOUR NAME HERE *(Do Not Print)*

Form **SS-5** (9-75)

☐ RESCREEN ☐ ASSIGN ☐ DUP ISSUED   Return completed application to nearest SOCIAL SECURITY ADMINISTRATION OFFICE

5. READING INFORMATION ON $1.00, $5.00, AND $10.00 BILLS

Using a one-, a five-, and a ten-dollar bill, answer the following:

a. Whose picture is on the front of the

(1) one-dollar bill? _____

(2) five-dollar bill? _____

(3) ten-dollar bill? _____

From *Reading for Survival in Today's Society*, Volume One, ©1978 Goodyear Publishing Company, Inc.

b. What is the name of the treasurer of the United States whose signature appears on the one-dollar bill?_____

_____

c. What series is the ten-dollar bill?_____

_____

d. What is the name of the secretary of the treasury whose signature appears on the five-dollar bill?_____

_____

e. What picture or pictures are on the back of the

(1) one-dollar bill? _____

_____

(2) five-dollar bill? _____

_____

(3) ten-dollar bill?_____

_____

f. What kind of note is each bill?_____

_____

g. What two separate sentences are printed on each bill?

(1) _____

_____

_____

(2) _____

_____

_____

From *Reading for Survival in Today's Society*, Volume One. ©1978 Goodyear Publishing Company, Inc.

other ideas

A. Using news magazines or newspapers, locate at least three articles where sums of tax dollars are reported as allocated for a certain use by the government. Below, list the reason for spending the money and the amount appropriated.

REASON FOR SPENDING TAX DOLLARS	AMOUNT APPROPRIATED

B. Write your congressman and ask to be placed on the mailing list for constituents.

C. Secure a copy of the *Congressional Record* from your congressman or by writing the Superintendent of Documents, U.S. Government Printing Office, Washington, D.C., 20405. Take particular notice of items *not* given coverage in the newspapers. In some instances, these items may be of interest to only a few people. What sort of items are these?

D. Write the U.S. Government Printing Office and request a list of publications dealing with some particular area of interest, such as a hobby, a vocation, or the like.

key words & phrases

federal	ballot	campaign	legislation
democracy	investigate	congress	capitalism
capitol	military	pledge	representative
citizen	welfare	committee	constituents
vote	regime	foreign	proceedings

From *Reading for Survival in Today's Society,* Volume One, ©1978 Goodyear Publishing Company, Inc.

self-evaluation

	date completed	possible score	your score	EXPERT	AVERAGE	FAIR	HELP!
1. Locating nearest regional address to request government information		6					
2. Noting directions to request government material		6					
3. Finding reports of government decisions		9					
4. Identifying key information on a social security card application form		14					
5. Reading information on $1.00, $5.00, and $10.00 bills		12					

CIRCLE **other ideas** COMPLETED: A B C D

TOTAL POSSIBLE POINTS: **47**

YOUR TOTAL POINTS:

How did you rate yourself?

name & date

From *Reading for Survival in Today's Society*, Volume One, ©1978 Goodyear Publishing Company, Inc.

composite
self-evaluation

	date completed	possible score	your score	EXPERT	AVERAGE	FAIR	HELP!
1. Labels		43		○	○	○	○
2. Printed Directions		48		○	○	○	○
3. Schedules		52		○	○	○	○
4. Magazine Facts		38		○	○	○	○
5. Current Events		32		○	○	○	○
6. Newspaper Classified Information		43		○	○	○	○
7. Weather Reports		49		○	○	○	○
8. Driver's Handbook		41		○	○	○	○
9. Signs		36		○	○	○	○
10. Maps		40		○	○	○	○
11. Travel Information		40		○	○	○	○
12. Dictionary		23		○	○	○	○
13. Telephone Directory		51		○	○	○	○
14. Job Application Forms		50		○	○	○	○
15. Bank Information		38		○	○	○	○
16. City Information		63		○	○	○	○
17. State Government Information		36		○	○	○	○
18. National Government Information		47		○	○	○	○

composite list of key words & phrases

The number in parentheses after the word or phrase indicates the module in which it appears.

a

A.M. (3)

abridged (12)

accelerate (8)

accommodations (11)

account (15)

add (2)

additive (1)

address (14)

adhere (2)

administrator (6)

advancement (6)

affix (12)

agency (17)

agriculture (4)

alphabetical (12)

altitude (7)

ambition (6)

anthropology (4)

area code (13)

arid (7)

arrive (3)

assessment (16)

assistance (13)

attended (14)

audit (17)

b

ballot (18)

banks (10)

benefits (6)

beverages (4)

beware (9)

birthdate (14)

births (5)

bonds (15)

book reviews (5)

budget (17)

c

campaign (18)

camping (4)

canal (10)

cancel (3)

cape (10)

capitalism (18)

capitol (18)

capsule (2)

cargo (3)

cartoon (5)

cashier (15)

caution (1)

Celsius (7)

chalet (11)

channel (10)

checking (15)

circulate (7)

citizen (18)

city hall (16)

classified (13)

climate (11)

clothing (4)

club meeting (5)

coin (15)

collect (13)

collision (8)

combine (2)

commerce (16)

commission (17)

committee (18)

complete (2)

complimentary (11)

compound (12)

compromise (17)

comptroller (16)

congress (18)

connection (3)

connotation (12)

constituents (18)

contents (1)

continental (11)

cottage (11)

county (17)

crosswalk (8)

currency (15)

curve (8)

custodian (16)

customer (13)

d

daily (1)

danger (9)

decorating (4)

deer crossing (9)

definition (12)

degree (14)

delicate (1)

democracy (18)

denotation (12)

depart (3)

department (17)

deposit (15)

derivation (12)

desert (10)

destination (11)

detour (10)

development (17)

diacritical (12)

dial (13)

dining (11)

diploma (14)

direct (3)

direct dial (13)

directory (13)

disability (14)

district (17)

dosage (1)

drizzle (7)

drought (7)

dry clean only (1)

dust-repellent (1)

duties (14)

e

editorials (5)

education (14)

electronics (4)

elevator (9)

emergency (13)

employee (17)

employer (6)

empty (2)

enlarge (2)

entertain (11)

entrance (9)

entry (12)

enumerate (2)

equator (10)

escalator (9)

escort (11)

etymology (12)

examiner (8)

executive (6)

exit (9)

expenses (11)

experience (6)

extended forecast (7)

extension (13)

extracurricular (14)

f

facilities (11)

Fahrenheit (7)

fare (3)

federal (18)

fire (16)

first class (3)

flight (3)

follow (2)

food (4)

for rent (9)

forecast (7)

foreign (18)

formula (1)

franchise (6)

freight (3)

funds (17)

g

games (4)

garage sale (9)

government (4)

governor (17)

graduate (6)

h

hazard (8)

high voltage (9)

historical site (17)

history (4)

homonym (12)

hospitality (11)

humidity (7)

i

illegal (8)

illustration (12)

immediately (6)

induce (1)

industry (4)

information (13)

inlet (10)

inquire (6)

installment (15)

institution (14)

interest (15)

internally (1)

international events (5)

intersection (8)

interstate (10)

investigate (18)

island (10)

k

key (10)

l

law (17)

lecture (5)

legislation (18)

library (16)

license (6)

loading zone (9)

loan (15)

local (13)

loiter (9)

luxurious (11)

m

mail delivery (5)

management (6)

manager (9)

marital (14)

mayor (16)

mechanical (4)

medicine (4)

merchant (16)

midnight (3)

military (18)

mist (7)

moisten (2)

motorist (8)

mouthpiece (13)

municipal (16)

music (4)

n

negotiable (15)

no hunting (9)

noon (3)

o

obituaries (5)

official (16)

one way (9)

operator (13)

opportunity (6)

p

P.M. (3)

page (17)

parallel (8)

park (17)

parking (16)

party (13)

passenger (3)

pedestrian (9)

peninsula (10)

permanent press (1)

person-to-person (13)

personalized (15)

pets (4)

photography (4)

planning (16)

pledge (18)

point (2)

police (16)

political decisions (5)

port (10)

position (6)

posted (9)

practical (14)

precaution (1)

precipitation (7)

prefix (12)

premier (5)

prescription (1)

present (2)

preservative (1)

press release (5)

pressure (7)

price change (5)

primary road (10)

print (2)

prior (2)

priority (3)

proceedings (18)

program (3)

pronunciation (12)

public (16)

puncture (1)

q

qualifications (14)

r

radio (5)

receiver (13)

recital (5)

recommendation (14)

reconstruct (17)

recreation (11)

reference (14)

regime (18)

relative (14)

release (2)

relevant (14)

remarks (2)

repair (6)

representative (18)

republic (10)

require (6)

reservation (11)

residence (13)

reverse (8)

rhyme (12)

right-of-way (8)

route (10)

rustic (11)

s

safe-deposit box (15)

sale (9)

sanitation (16)

savings (15)

school (16)

scientific (4)

seal (2)

secondary road (17)

security (15)

service charge (15)

services (3)

shoulder (8)

showers (7)

sightseer (11)

sign (2)

signal (8)

siren (8)

skid (8)

skilled (6)

sound (10)

sports (5)

spouse (14)

static (7)

station-to-station (13)

stationary (7)

status (14)

steer (8)

strait (10)

street (16)

suffix (12)

supervisor (6)

survey (17)

swamp (10)

sweltering (7)

syllables (12)

synonym (12)

synthetic (1)

t

take (2)

taxes (17)

teeth (4)

telecommunication (13)

television (5)

teller (15)

temperature (7)

theater (5)

timed (2)

title (14)

toll road (10)

tools (4)

tornado (7)

torrent (7)

tourist class (3)

training (6)

transaction (15)

trespassing (9)

trial (5)

u

update (5)

upgrade (8)

urban (16)

usage (1)

v

vacancy (9)

vacation (11)

variant (12)

vault (15)

vehicle (8)

ventilation (1)

via (3)

villa (11)

violation (8)

vote (18)

w

warning (1)

water treatment (16)

welfare (18)

withdrawal (15)

answer
key

Module 1. LABELS

1. a. January 1980.
   b. Four.
   c. On the package insert (inside).
   d. Yes. It is required by federal law.
2. a. (1) Bathroom.
      (2) Kitchen.
   b. (1) Cleans.
      (2) Brightens.
      (3) Disinfects.
   c. They may not stay as white and bright as possible.
   d. (1) Blood.
      (2) Berries.
      (3) Perspiration stains.
3. a. Milk.
   b. Flood the eyes with water.
   c. (1) Ammonia.
      (2) Acid.
   d. No. It could be mistaken for Clorox. (Answers to second part may vary.)
   e. ½ cup.
   f. Keep out of reach of children.
   g. ¾ cup.
   h. Cork.
4. a. 4½ ounces.
   b. My*T*Fine.
   c. Chocolate.
   d. Pudding.
   e. No.
5. Net Weight: 4½ ounces; 46 fluid ounces.
   Ingredients: artificial chocolate flavor; artificial coloring.
   Company Name: not shown; RJR Foods, Inc.
   City and State: not shown; Winston-Salem, N.C.
   Product Name: My*T*Fine Instant Pudding; Hawaiian Punch Fruit Punch.
   Flavor: chocolate; fruit juicy red.
   Calories: not shown; 90.

Module 2. PRINTED DIRECTIONS

1. a. Nonmetal.
   b. Water.
   c. 4 servings: 2 scoops.
      1 gallon: 8 scoops.
      1 serving: ½ scoop.
      2 quarts: 4 scoops.
   d. 8 quarts.

2. a. Add water.
   b. Beat the eggs.
   c. **2** tablespoons of oil and ⅓ cup egg mixture.
   d. You supply the eggs.
3. a. (1) Print.
      (2) Write your first name, then your initial, then last name.
   b. 2.
   c. Complete the blank if you have changed employers within 2 years.
   d. Give your driver license number and state.
   e. (1) Person name.
      (2) Company name.
      (3) Insurance amount.
      (4) Date.
      (5) Reason.
4. Answers will vary, with the exception of those facts furnished in the instructions.
5. Answers will vary.

Module 3. SCHEDULES

1. a. 12:05 P.M.
   b. 10:02 P.M.
   c. 7:35 P.M.
   d. The flight from Miami to Seattle / Tacoma.
   e. Three.
   f. **7:11 A.M.:** 4 hours, 21 minutes.
      3:10 P.M.: 4 hours, 33 minutes.
2. a. The flight to Honolulu.
   b. The flight to Hartford.
   c. (1) 836
      (2) 956
      (3) 972
   d. The flight from Miami to Pittsburgh.
   e. Saturday and Sunday only.
   f. **Departs:** 10:00 P.M.; **Arrives:** 12:27 A.M.
      Departs: 8:10 P.M.; **Arrives:** 1:37 A.M.
3. a. One or more.
      Beneath the seat or in an approved carry-on compartment.
   b. $10.00.
   c. (1) Hearing aid.
      (2) Heart pacemaker.
   d. Answers will vary. Sample answers are:
      (1) American Express.
      (2) BankAmericard.
      (3) Mastercharge.
   e. Your name and address.
   f. $500.

g. (1) Acid.
   (2) Matches.
   (3) Lighter fluid.
   (4) Hazardous articles.
4. a. Denver to New York/Newark: $186.
   Omaha to San Diego: $168.
   Boston to Salt Lake City: $230.
   Washington, D.C., to Atlanta: $86.
b. (1) $105.
   (2) $81.
   (3) $45.
   (4) $84.
   Total: $315.
5. a. "Somerset"
b. "The A.M. Show"
c. "Stranded"
d. Channel 4
e. "Magnificent Marble Machine"
f. Answers will vary. Sample answers are:
   (1) "Captain Kangaroo"
   (2) "Good Morning, America"
   (3) "Baretta"
   (4) "Sanford and Son"
   (5) "The Price Is Right"
g. Answers will vary.

Module 4. MAGAZINE FACTS

1. Answers will vary.
2. a. 10.
b. $6.95 plus shipping and handling.
c. Return the book within 10 days.
d. Time-Life *Encyclopedia of Gardening*.
e. When? At any time.
   How? By notifying the company.
3. a. Two.
b. Cloth.
c. Three.
d. Drinking straw.
e. Two drops of Elmer's glue.
f. Elmer's.
g. Elmer's
   P.O. Box 25W
   Hilliard, Ohio 43026
4. Answers will vary.
5. Answers will vary.

Module 5. CURRENT EVENTS

Answers will vary.

Module 6. NEWSPAPER CLASSIFIED INFORMATION

1. Answers will vary.
2. a. 1972 Harley-Davidson Sportster at $2300.
  b. 1971 Honda and 1972 Suzuki dirt bike at $350.
  c. 1965 Harley-Davidson Chopper.
  d. 1973 Honda CB 350.
  e. 383-7080.
  f. 1970 Honda 350.
  g. Harley-Davidson and Yamaha.
  h. After 5:30.
3. a. 477-1070.
  b. Villa Apartments.
  c. 683-1541.
  d. Bath and shower, walk-in closet, off-street parking.
  e. 493-1481.
     No.
4. a. McBroom's Rentals.
  b. 682-6498, 477-8662, 477-2923, 489-8269.
  c. 596-5166.
  d. 477-6176.
  e. 688-6973.
5. Answers will vary.

Module 7. WEATHER REPORTS

1. a. 10 percent.
  b. **High**, 58; **low**, 36.
  c. 66 degrees.
  d. Page 2A.
2. a. (1) Mid-60s.
     (2) 45 to 52 today, 50 to 58 Friday.
     (3) 58 to 64.
     (4) 62 to 72 in upper deserts, 74 to 80 in lower
         deserts.
     (5) Mid to upper 60s.
  b. 2 degrees higher.
  c. Little or no smog.
  d. 8 to 18.
3. a. **Mountains:** upper 20s to middle 30s.
     Beaches: middle 30s to low 40s.
  b. (1) 25 degrees.
     (2) 26 degrees.
     (3) 26 degrees.
     (4) 29 degrees.
     (5) 22 degrees.
     (6) 21 degrees.
     (7) 26 degrees.
     (8) 25 degrees.
  c. 37 percent.

    d. Homestead, Florida.
    e. Bradford, Pennsylvania.
4. a. Eureka.
    b. Any two:
      (1) Nevada.
      (2) Oregon.
      (3) Washington.
      (4) Idaho.
      (5) Kansas.
      (6) Nebraska.
      (7) Florida.
    c. Corpus Christi.
    d. (1) Charleston.
      (2) Jacksonville.
      (3) Miami.
    e. Cold.
    f. West.
    g. A low pressure zone.
    h. It was clear.
5. a. Blythe, Needles, and Palm Springs.
    b. Long Beach.
    c. Six.
    d. (1) 17 degrees.
      (2) 23 degrees.
      (3) 31 degrees.
      (4) 30 degrees.
      (5) 14 degrees.
      (6) 21 degrees.
    e. San Antonio.
      Des Moines.
    f. **Coolest:** Amsterdam.
      Warmest: New Delhi.

Module 8. DRIVER'S HANDBOOK

1. Answers may vary. Sample definitions are:
    a. A license obtained when one granted previously
      expires.
    b. Right of passage.
    c. A road that runs across two or more states.
    d. Danger; unsafe obstacle or condition.
    e. Situation that presents an urgent need.
    f. Unpaved but usually flat area on either side of a road.
    g. Person who is walking.
    h. Divider between opposite lanes of traffic.
2. a. 15 points.
    b. His license might be suspended or revoked, and he
      could be fined or imprisoned.
    c. He could complete a course at a driver education
      clinic.

3. Reading down from the top:
   Left-hand column
   Approaching divided highway.
   Divided highway ends.
   Yield right-of-way.
   No right turns.
   No U-turns.
   Deer crossing.
   Keep right.
   Do not enter.
   No trucks.
   Right-hand column
   Hill; steep grade.
   Do not pass when yellow line is in your lane.
   Road slippery when wet.
   Pedestrian crossing.
   12-foot 6-inch clearance under bridge or overpass.
   Signal light.
   Traffic entering main highway.
   Two-way traffic.
   School crossing.
4. a. Remain stopped.
   Paragraph: 3.
   b. Special signals.
   Paragraph: 5.
   c. Pedestrians.
   Paragraph: 2.
   d. Remain stopped until he is across.
   Paragraph: 4.
5. a. 243
   b. 88
   c. 66
   366

Module 9. SIGNS

1. a. C
   b. E
   c. A, D
   d. B
   e. C
   f. To the right.
   g. To the left.
   h. One.
2. a. Exit.
   b. Barber or beauty shop.
   c. Men's restroom.
   d. Post office.
   e. Women's restroom.
   f. Entrance.

3. a. D
  b. C
  c. B
  d. A
  e. (1) 9-9
    (2) 9-6
    (3) 1-6
4. a. (1) A
    (2) C
  b. (1) B
    (2) E
  c. (1) B
    (2) D
  d. C
5. a. C, F
  b. C or F
  c. A, B, or D
  d. C, E, and F

Module 10. MAPS

1. a. P, 6-D
  b. W1, 3-F
  c. T, 2-L
  d. B, 3-L
  e. D, 4-E
2. a. (1) 70 or I-85
    (2) 15 or I-85
    (3) 70
    (4) 15-501
  b. (1) 751
    (2) 501
    (3) 55
3. a. Sleepy Time Inn.
  b. Chesterfield Motel.
  c. (1) Governors Inn.
    (2) Triangle Motel.
  d. Any two:
    (1) Duke Street.
    (2) Pettigrew Street.
    (3) Chapel Hill Street.
    (4) Mangum Street.
  e. (1) Lawson Street.
    (2) Fayetteville Street.
4. a. Markham.
  b. NC 751.
  c. Chapel Hill;
    Duke University.
  d. Carver Street.
  e. Carver Street.

5. a. Pacific.
   b. Eastern.
   c. Eastern.
   d. Eastern.
   e. Pacific.
   f. Central.
   g. Central.
   h. Eastern.
   i. Pacific.

Module 11. TRAVEL INFORMATION

1. a. 4 days and 3 nights.
   b. No.
   c. **Double:** with terrace.
      Triple: in suite.
   d. Subcompact automatic-shift car.
   e. 15¢ per mile.
   f. No.
2. a. (1) Fact.
      (2) Opinion.
      (3) Fact.
      (4) Opinion.
      (5) Opinion.
   b. Answers will vary.
3. a. Hilton Inn South.
   b. Red Carpet Inn International.
   c. Motor Inn Plaza Hotels.
   d. Red Carpet Inn International.
   e. $109.83.
   f. No.
   g. $8.50.
4. a. Daytona Beach.
   b. (1) Sarasota.
      (2) Colony Beach Resort.
   c. From September 9 to December 15.
   d. $2.95.
   e. Answers will vary.
5. a. (1) By tour guide tape player.
      (2) (a) Flock.
          (b) Pride.
      (3) (a) Roll up all windows.
          (b) Lock all doors.
      (4) Answers will vary. Possible answers are:
          Because a giraffe is so tall that, as you look out your
          car window at one, you will be looking directly at his knees.
          Because a giraffe is so tall that, as you sit
          in your car and look out, your eyes will be the same
          distance above the ground as his knees.
      (5) (a) Lions.
          (b) Cheetahs.

    b. (1) (a) Jeeps.
           (b) Pedal boats.
           (c) Train.
     (2) No.
     (3) Close-enough-to-touch.
     (4) More colorful.

Module 12. DICTIONARY

1. Answers will vary.
2. Answers will vary.
3. a. A fringe of hair combed or brushed forward over the forehead.
   b. To strike or beat resoundingly.
   c. A loud, sudden, explosive noise.
   d. Answers will vary.
4. a. Banker.
   b. Bankhead.
   c. Bank balance.
   d. Bank holiday.
   e. Bank loan.
   f. Bank night.
   g. Bank clerk or banker.
5. bane: bandleader. (The word is **baneberry**.)
   banj: bank night. (The word is **banjo**.)
   bani: bank night. (The word is **banister**.)
   band: bandleader. (The object is a **band saw**.)
   band: bandleader. (The word is **bandy**.)

Module 13. TELEPHONE DIRECTORY

1. a. (1) 911
     (2) 682-5617 or 372-5485
     (3) 911
     (4) 911
     (5) 911
     (6) 684-8111
     (7) 372-0711
     (8) 683-2521
   b. Exactly where help is needed.
   c. Any numbers you might need in an emergency, such as your doctor's number.
   d. No answers required.
2. a. 805
   b. 804
   c. 904
   d. 717
   e. 616
   f. 808
   g. 713

h. 518
i. 216
j. 307
k. 317
l. 316
m. 404
n. 303
o. 918

3. **a.** 419-2084
   b. 1213 North Duke
   c. 419-3701
   d. From 11:00 A.M. to 12:00 P.M. Monday through Thursday; from 11:00 A.M. to 1:00 A.M. Friday and Saturday.
   e. (1) Great prices.
      (2) Good meals.
   f. No.
   g. Villa Dinner Theatre, 419-2308.
   h. President's Room.

4. Answers will vary.

5. **a.** Attorney or lawyer.
   b. 616 Granby.
   c. Thomas.
   d. (1) 590-0505
      (2) 590-4560
      (3) 590-8175
      (4) 329-2440
      (5) 590-2134

Module 14. JOB APPLICATION FORMS

1. Answers will vary.
2. Answers may vary. Sample definitions are:
   a. Employment status; job.
   b. Inhabitant of a particular city, state, or country.
   c. Employment history; jobs held previously.
   d. Of late.
   e. Testimonials and/or opinions concerning a person's character, experience, qualifications, etc.
   f. Person applying for a job.
   g. Person's name written by that person.
   h. Medical history, including severe illnesses, injuries, or disabilities, particularly those that might hinder job performance.
   i. Person for whom the applicant is now working.
   j. Wages, money earned.
3. Answers will vary.
4. Answers will vary.
5. Answers will vary.

Module 15. BANK INFORMATION

1. Answers will vary. Sample definitions are:
   a. A written order to a bank to pay money.
   b. Record of your signature kept by a bank for purposes of comparison and verification.
   c. Addition of money to an account.
   d. Any negotiation; any act of banking business in which money is deposited, withdrawn, or exchanged.
   e. Money deposited to earn interest dividends.
   f. Money deposited for easy access and used or withdrawn by writing checks.
   g. Paper money.
   h. The mean or normal amount of money kept in an account.
   i. Sign.
   j. An amount of money large enough to meet bank requirements or to cover checks drawn on the account.
2. a. $20,000.
   b. 1-234-567.
   c. (1) The second set of imprinted numbers.
      (2) On the bottom edge of the check.
   d. Magnetic ink.
   e. On the bottom edge and/or the upper right corner.
   f. $100.
3. a. Don't.
   b. Do.
   c. Don't.
   d. Don't.
   e. Do.
   f. Don't.
4. a. At the top.
   b. (1) In figures.
      (2) In letters (words).
   c. At the bottom.
   d. (1) Account number.
      (2) Name.
      (3) Date.
   e. $134.32 (total).
   f. (1) Make up your mind to save.
      (2) Have an objective.
      (3) Save systematically and regularly.
   g. 5 percent.
5. a. The account number.
   b. A check for the opening deposit.
   c. Answers will vary.

Module 16. CITY INFORMATION

1. **a.** 30 days.
   b. 299.
   c. 24.
   d. 549-8221.
   e. Delta, Eastern, Piedmont, United, and two commuter airlines.
   f. 688-4587.
   g. 35,000.
   h. 1,500,000.
   i. 116.69 square miles.
   j. commercial and industrial
   k. (1) I-70
     (2) I-25
2. **a.** Riverview
   b. College Plaza.
   c. Wellons Village.
   d. (1) Arlans Plaza.
     (2) University.
     (3) Westfield.
   e. Northgate.
   f. (1) Street.
     (2) Avenue.
     (3) Junior.
     (4) And.
     (5) Boulevard.
     (6) East.
     (7) Square feet.
     (8) Post office.
     (9) Interstate 85.
     (10) Road.
3. Answers will vary.
4. Answers will vary.
5. Answers will vary.

Module 17. STATE GOVERNMENT INFORMATION

1. Answers will vary. Sample definitions are:
   a. Immunity; something for which one is not liable.
   b. One who is supported financially by someone else.
   c. Property, real or personal; total liabilities and assets of a bankrupt or deceased person.
   d. An amount subtracted.
   e. Someone who lives in a particular place.
   f. Something that is voluntarily given or paid to a charitable organization.
   g. Total amount of earnings.

2. a. (1) What is Katherine Williams's county of residence?
(2) Did she file a 1974 North Carolina return?
(3) Was she a legal resident of North Carolina
during the entire year of 1975?
(4) What is her employer's address?
(5) How much North Carolina tax has been withheld from her earnings?
(See item 17.)

   b. (1) Top of the form.
(2) Beside the signature.

3. a. $1000
   b. $1000
   c. $2000
   d. $600
   e. Answers will vary. Sample answers are:
(1) Business college.
(2) Beauty school.
(3) Technical institute.
   f. 183

4. a. In the House.
   b. Answers will vary. Sample answers are:
(1) Presentation.
(2) Committee consideration.
(3) Voting.
   c. Senate.
   d. Three.
   e. House.
   f. Any two:
(1) Enrollment.
(2) Further consideration by House.
(3) Sent to conference committee.
(4) Failure.
   g. Sign the bill or fail to sign it but not veto it.
   h. *Oregon Revised Statutes* or *Session Laws*.

5. a. Answers will vary.
   b. Tractors.
   c. Two.
   d. Motorcycle drivers and riders must wear protective
safety helmets.
   e. Yes.
   f. Answers will vary.

Module 18. NATIONAL GOVERNMENT INFORMATION

1. **a.** Answers will vary.
   b. Dallas, Texas.
   c. Burlington, Massachusetts.
   d. Information Division
   e. (1) 1100 Commerce Street
   (2) Room 5-D-22
2. **a.** Superintendent of Documents
   U.S. Government Printing Office
   Washington, D.C., 20402
   b. No (unless a price is indicated).
   c. (1) Explanation of the need for the materials.
   (2) Explanation of how they will be used.
   d. (1) Title of the publication.
   (2) Series number of the publication.
3. Answers will vary.
4. Answers will vary.
5. **a.** (1) George Washington
   (2) Abraham Lincoln
   (3) Alexander Hamilton
   b-d. Answers will vary, according to the date each
   bill was printed.
   e. (1) The Great Seal of the United States.
   (2) The Lincoln Memorial.
   (3) The U.S. Treasury.
   f. Federal Reserve note.
   g. (1) In God we trust.
   (2) This note is legal tender for all debts,
   public and private.